CHINESE
CHARACTERS
WRITING PRACTICE PAD

XIN LIANG AND MARTHA LAM

TUTTLE Publishing

Tokyo │Rutland, Vermont│ Singapore

Published by Tuttle Publishing, an imprint of Periplus Editions (HK) Ltd.

www.tuttlepublishing.com

Copyright © 2022 by Periplus Editions (HK) Ltd

ISBN 978-0-8048-4678-3

Distributed by

North America, Latin America & Europe
Tuttle Publishing
364 Innovation Drive, North Clarendon
VT 05759-9436 U.S.A.
Tel: 1 (802) 773-8930
Fax: 1 (802) 773-6993
info@tuttlepublishing.com
www.tuttlepublishing.com

Japan
Tuttle Publishing
Yaekari Building, 3rd Floor, 5-4-12 Osaki,
Shinagawa-ku, Tokyo 141 0032
Tel: (81) 3 5437-0171
Fax: (81) 3 5437-0755
sales@tuttle.co.jp
www.tuttle.co.jp

Asia Pacific
Berkeley Books Pte. Ltd.
3 Kallang Sector #04-01, Singapore 349278
Tel: (65) 6741-2178
Fax: (65) 6741-2179
inquiries@periplus.com.sg
www.tuttlepublishing.com

26 25 24 23 22
10 9 8 7 6 5 4 3 2 1   2112EP

Printed in China

INTRODUCTION

How did characters come about?

Chinese characters, or Hanzi (汉字), have evolved over 5,000 years. While the earliest characters inscribed on oracle bones (1600–1046 B.C.) are mostly pictographic (象形), they only represent about 4% of the total number. The vast majority are pictophonetic characters (形声), consisting of a meaning and a phonetic component. The other two categories include indicative characters (指示) and associative characters (会意). Below are examples of the four categories:

Pictographic characters 象形字	Originally resemble the objects they represent	山 *mountain* 山		
		雨 *rain* 雨		
Pictophonetic characters 形声字	Contain two parts, one indicates the sound and the other conveys the meaning	妈 *mother*	女 *meaning* +	马 *sound*
Indicative characters 指示字	Pictures of ideas	一 *one*	二 *two*	上 *up* 下 *down*
Associative characters 会意字	Combine two or more existing characters to indicate new meaning	好 *good*	女 *daughter* +	子 *son*
		In Chinese culture, having a son and a daughter is good.		

How are characters pronounced?

Chinese is not a phonetic language and the romanization of a character usually bears no relation to its written form. This book adopts the Hanyu Pinyin, a special romanization system, created for learners of Chinese to aid pronunciation. Each Chinese character is pronounced using only one syllable. A syllable consists of an initial consonant, a final vowel, and a tone. Here is an example of the syllable **mā**.

Chinese is a tonal language. Tone matters because a variation in tone implies a change in meaning. There are four main tones, plus a neutral tone, and each tone is marked by an accent over the vowel.

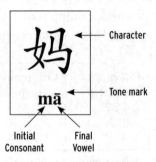

1st tone	high, flat	**mā**	妈 *mother*
2nd tone	rising	**má**	麻 *linen*
3rd tone	down-up	**mǎ**	马 *horse*
4th tone	falling	**mà**	骂 *scold*
Neutral tone	soft	**ma**	吗 *Yes/no question marker*

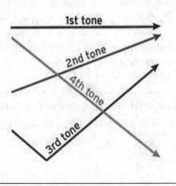

How do I write Chinese characters?

Chinese characters are squarish in appearance. In learning to write the characters try to visualize them as in a box each, and the proper rendering of each stroke should result in a neat character well proportioned and "sitting" right in the middle of the invisible box.

Basic strokes Each character is composed of a number of basic strokes. Strokes come in various shapes and sizes: a stroke can be a dot, a horizontal line, a vertical line, a diagonal line or a line with a hook. The basic eight strokes are indicated in the character 永:

Dash
Héng
横

Dot
Diǎn
点

Left-falling
stroke
Piě
撇

Right-rising
stroke
Tí
提

Right-falling
stroke
Nà
捺

Twist
Wān
弯

Hook
Gōu
钩

Straight-down
stroke
Shù
竖

Stroke order Writing characters in the correct stroke order is important if the character is to have the correct appearance. To get it right, it is important to remember the 7 rules:

Rule 1	From top to bottom	一 二
Rule 2	From left to right	丿 亻 仁 仁
Rule 3	Horizontal before vertical	一 十 土
Rule 4	Downward-left before downward-right	丿 人
Rule 5	Outside before inside	丶 厂 门 闪 闪
Rule 6	Inside before closing the bottom	丨 冂 冋 冋 冋 回
Rule 7	Middle before two sides	亅 小 小

Radicals Every Chinese character has a radical or is itself a radical. There are more than 200 radicals in Chinese. Take a look at these three characters:

nǐ   **tā**   **zhù**
你 (*you*)   他 (*he/him*)   住 (*live*)

They have the same component 亻 on the left-hand side. 亻 is 人, which means a person. This component 亻 is the radical for all the three characters above and it gives a clue to the meaning of the character.

Knowing radicals not only helps us to guess the meaning of a character, but it also makes it easy for us to look up the meaning of a character in a dictionary. A radical list is included on pages xiv to xvi to facilitate your learning of the radicals.

What are the main characteristics of Chinese grammar?

Word order plays a key role in structuring ideas. The word order of the basic Chinese sentence structure is "Subject–Verb–Object," which matches that of English (see Example 1). A question in Chinese follows the same word order of a statement (see Example.2).

Example	Subject	Verb	Object
1.	**Wǒ** 我 I	**xué** 学 study	**Zhōngwén.** 中文。 Chinese
	I study Chinese.		
2.	**Nǐ** 你 you	**xué** 学 study	**shénme?** 什么？ what
	What do you study?		

The significance of the word order emerges as we try to add more details to the basic sentence structure. For example, the notion of place goes before the verb (see Example 3).

Example	Subject	Place	Verb	Object
3.	**Wǒ** 我 I	**zài Běijīng** 在北京 in Beijing	**xué** 学 study	**Zhōngwén.** 中文。 Chinese
	I studied Chinese in Beijing.			

If we add a time notion to the above sentence, we can either put Time before Place (see Example 4) or put Time at the beginning of the sentence (see Example 5).

Example	Subject	Time	Place	Verb	Object
4.	**Wǒ** 我 I	**qùnián** 去年 last year	**zài Běijīng** 在北京 in Beijing	**xué** 学 study	**Zhōngwén.** 中文。 Chinese
	I studied Chinese in Beijing last year.				
5.	**Qùnián** 去年 Last year	**wǒ** 我 I	**zài Běijīng** 在北京 in Beijing	**xué** 学 study	**Zhōngwén.** 中文。 Chinese
	I studied Chinese in Beijing last year.				

There are always exceptions to the word order, depending on the different grammatical functions and the complexity of the sentence. For beginners, the above basic structures should suffice.

Function words (虚词) play an important role in a sentence and unlike English, Chinese is not an inflectional language. The verb-form remains unchanged under all circumstances, and function words are added to indicate the subtle changes in meaning. Function words serve only grammatical functions and they often carry no meaning by themselves. They appear as adverbs, prepositions, conjunctions and particles, interjections and onomatopoeias.

For example, the function word 了 **le** is used to indicate past action.

Wǒ qù Běijīng.	vs	**Wǒ qù Běijīng le.**
我 去北京。		我 去北京 了。
I go to Beijing.		I went to Beijing.

The function word 在 **zài** is used as a preposition in the example below:

Wǒ zài Běijīng xué Zhōngwén
我 在 北京 学 中文。
I study Chinese in Beijing.

The Chinese language does not have tenses: the same verb 去 can be used for today, tomorrow or yesterday. To depict tenses, function words and other words can be used.

For example, if you want to say "I go to Beijing today," then the word 今天 ("today") can be used to indicate the tense, as given below:

Wǒ   jīntiān   qù   Běijīng.

我　　今天　　去　北京。

I go to Beijing today.

If you want to say "I went to Beijing," then the word 了 (a particle) is used to indicate a past action, as follows:

Wǒ   qù   Běijīng   le.

我　去　北京　了。

I went to Beijing.

If you want to say "I will go to Beijing tomorrow," the word 明天 ("tomorrow") is used to indicate future tense:

Wǒ   míngtiān   qù   Běijīng.

我　明天　　去　北京

I will go to Beijing tomorrow.

How to use the Practice Pad?

1. There are 280 main characters, which cover the basic characters required for the levels 1 and 2 of **Hànyǔ Shuǐpíng Kǎoshì** (HSK). It is an international standardized examination that tests and rates Chinese language proficiency. Some characters are also chosen from HSK levels 3 and 4 because of their high-frequency usage in daily communication.

2. One good way to learn characters is to practice writing every day, especially if you think about what each character means as you write it. If you are working on your own without a teacher, work through only a few characters at a time.

3. The front of each page shows a single character, its pronunciation and English meaning. Where the traditional form differs from the simplified form, it is shown on the page. You should try to memorize the shape, sound and meaning of each character as a whole.

   The stroke order guide and the direction of each stroke are given just above the character. They show you the correct way to write each character and you can use the blank boxes to practice writing the character.

   Common words or phrases give examples of how the character is combined with other character(s) to make words. These common words or phrases are chosen because they are everyday words that are frequently used by Chinese speakers, and they are taken from HSK Levels 1–3.

4. To help you use the main character, a short dialogue in Chinese, with pinyin romanization and English meaning, is displayed on the back of the page. The dialogue illustrates how the character and the main words are used in daily communication. The topics also include most language functions required at HSK levels 1 and 2.

Front of page

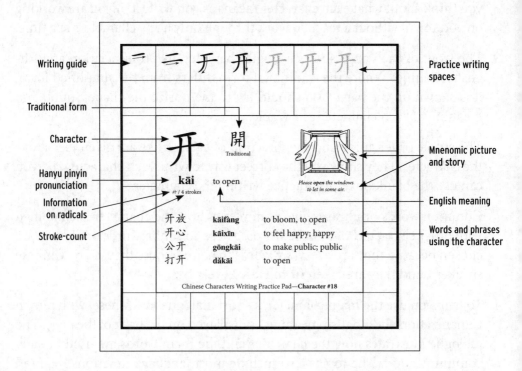

Writing guide →

← **Practice writing spaces**

Traditional form —

Character →

开

開
Traditional

Hanyu pinyin pronunciation → **kāi**

Information on radicals → 廾 / 4 strokes

Stroke-count —

to open

Please open the windows to let in some air.

← **Mnemonic picture and story**

← **English meaning**

开放	kāifàng	to bloom, to open
开心	kāixīn	to feel happy; happy
公开	gōngkāi	to make public; public
打开	dǎkāi	to open

← **Words and phrases using the character**

Chinese Characters Writing Practice Pad—**Character #18**

xii

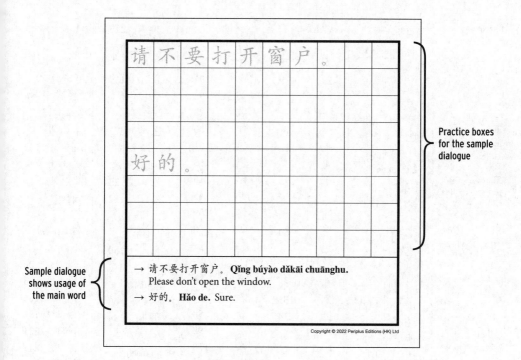

请 不 要 打 开 窗 户。

好 的。

→ 请不要打开窗户。 **Qǐng búyào dǎkāi chuānghu.**
Please don't open the window.
→ 好的。 **Hǎo de.** Sure.

Practice boxes for the sample dialogue

Sample dialogue shows usage of the main word

LIST OF RADICALS

1 stroke

[、]
为 262

[一]
七 2
不 3
一 4
下 8
三 9
面 51
上 67
东 167
两 199

[丨]
中 52

[丶]
事 272

[丿]
么 13
九 19
年 144
乐 246

[一]
书 73

[乙]
买 60
习 61
也 211

2 strokes

[冫]
冷 128

[亠]
离 209

[讠]
请 42
说 50
话 71
认 107
识 108
语 109
读 111
课 186
试 270
让 274

[二]
二 77
五 78
些 79

[十]
十 1
午 17
卖 235
千 275

[匚]
医 64

[刂]
前 38
别 155
到 234

[冖]
写 119

[冂]
再 118
肉 212

[亻]
住 44
什 53
他 91
们 92
做 93
作 100
你 101
便 153
体 215
件 245
休 259
但 280

[人]
个 66
人 87
今 88
会 98
从 178
以 223

[八]
八 114
六 115
公 189
共 193

真 225

[刀]
分 139

[夕]
色 273

[儿]
儿 25
先 112

[几]
几 130

[阝(left)]
院 68
阴 194

[阝(right)]
都 14
那 105

[力]
动 173
助 253

[又]
友 54

[厶]
去 86

[凵]
出 162

[匕]
北 15

3 strokes

[氵]
汉 20
没 23
游 184
汽 185
洗 221
泳 249

[忄]
懂 192
快 195
慢 203
忙 207
情 240

十 十 十 十

十

shí   ten, 10

十 / 2 strokes

I can form a 10 with two sticks.

十分	**shífēn**	completely, a hundred percent
十二	**shíèr**	twelve, 12
十月	**Shíyuè**	October
十个人	**shí gè rén**	ten persons

Chinese Characters Writing Practice Pad—**Character #1**

几 个 人 ?

十 个 。

→ 几个人? **Jǐ gè rén?** How many people?
→ 十个。 **Shí gè.** 10 people.

七　七　七　七　七

七

qī　　　seven, 7

一 / 2 strokes

*A rainbow has **seven** colors.*

七月　　　**Qīyuè**　　July
七十　　　**qīshí**　　seventy, 70
十七　　　**shíqī**　　seventeen, 17
七喜　　　**qīxǐ**　　7 Up (soft drink)

Chinese Characters Writing Practice Pad—**Character #2**

你 几 岁 ?

十 七 。

→ 你几岁? **Nǐ jǐ suì?** How old are you?

→ 十七。 **Shíqī.** Seventeen.

一 | 丆 | 不 | 不 | 不 | 不 | 不

不

bù/bú   not, no

一 / 4 strokes

No

*We shake our heads to say "**No.**"*

不是	**búshì**	no, is not, not
不用	**búyòng**	need not
不客气	**bú kèqi**	it's my pleasure
不管	**bùguǎn**	no matter, regardless of

Chinese Characters Writing Practice Pad—**Character #3**

谢	谢	你	。						
不	客	气	。						

→ 谢谢你。 **Xièxie nǐ.** Thank you.

→ 不客气。 **Bú kèqi.** It's my pleasure.

一

yī one
一 / 1 stroke

*To answer to "how many," we can put out a finger to say "**one**."*

一个	**yí gè**	one (item)
一起	**yìqǐ**	together
第一	**dì-yī**	first, number one
一点	**yìdiǎn**	a bit

Chinese Characters Writing Practice Pad—**Character #4**

多吃一点吧。

吃饱了。

→ 多吃一点吧。 **Duō chī yìdiǎn ba.** Have a bit more.

→ 吃饱了。 **Chī bǎo le.** I'm full.

`	`ᴗ	宀	宁	字	字	字	字
字							

字

zì   character, word

子 / 6 strokes

*These **words** mean "Thank you" in Chinese.*

名字	**míngzi**	name
字母	**zìmǔ**	letter (of the alphabet)
字典	**zìdiǎn**	dictionary
汉字	**Hànzì**	Chinese character
打字	**dǎzì**	to type

Chinese Characters Writing Practice Pad—**Character #5**

你	叫	什	么	名	字	？			
我	姓	李	，		叫	小	东	。	

→ 你叫什么名字？ **Nǐ jiào shénme míngzi?**
What is your name?

→ 我姓李，叫小东。 **Wǒ xìng Lǐ, jiào Xiǎodōng.**
My surname is Li, my name is Xiao Dong.

亻	乍	仁	仁	乍	乍	怎	怎
怎	怎	怎	怎				

怎

zěn　　how

心 / 9 strokes

$(10 \div 5) \times 2 - 4 + 6$

?

*I don't know **how** to do this math sum.*

怎样	**zěnyàng**	how, why?
怎么	**zěnme**	what?
怎么办	**zěnme bàn**	What can we do?
怎么样	**zěnmeyàng**	What's the matter?

Chinese Characters Writing Practice Pad—**Character #6**

怎	么	办	？						
我	不	知	道	！					

→ 怎么办？ **Zěnme bàn?** What can we do?

→ 我不知道！ **Wǒ bù zhīdào!** I don't know!

丨 冂 冃 冃 用 国 国 国

国 国 国

国
國
Traditional

guó country, nation
口 / 8 strokes

INDIA

India is an independent country.

国家 **guójiā** country, nation
国际 **guójì** international
中国 **Zhōngguó** China
外国 **wàiguó** foreign country

Chinese Characters Writing Practice Pad—**Character #7**

你	是	哪	国	人	？				
我	是	美	国	人	。				

→ 你是哪国人？ **Nǐ shì nǎ guó rén?** What's your nationality?

→ 我是美国人。 **Wǒ shì Měiguó rén.** I am American.

一　下　下　下　下　下

下

xià　　down

一 / 3 strokes

The roots of plants grow **down**wards.

下午	**xiàwǔ**	afternoon
下班	**xiàbān**	to get off work
一下	**yíxià**	a bit, a little
坐下	**zuòxia**	to sit down

Chinese Characters Writing Practice Pad—**Character #8**

休	息	一	下	吧	。				
谢	谢	。							

→ 休息一下吧。 **Xiūxi yíxià ba.** Please take a break.

→ 谢谢。 **Xièxie.** Thanks.

三　　三　　三　　三　　三　　三

三

sān　　three, 3

一 / 3 strokes

*A tripod stand has **three** legs.*

三十	**sānshí**	thirty, 30
星期三	**Xīngqī sān**	Wednesday
三明治	**sānmíngzhì**	sandwich
三角	**sānjiǎo**	triangle

Chinese Characters Writing Practice Pad—**Character #9**

吃 什 么 ？

三 明 治 。

→ 吃什么？ **Chī shénme?** What do you want to eat?
→ 三明治。 **Sānmíngzhì.** A sandwich.

丨	冂	曰	旦	旦	甲	畀	果
果	果	果					

果

guǒ　fruit

木 / 8 strokes

*Someone sent me a basket of **fruits**.*

水果　　**shuǐguǒ**　　fruit
苹果　　**píngguǒ**　　apple
果汁　　**guǒzhī**　　fruit juice
如果　　**rúguǒ**　　if

Chinese Characters Writing Practice Pad—**Character #10**

你喝什么？

一杯苹果汁。

→ 你喝什么？ **Nǐ hē shénme?** What do you want to drink?

→ 一杯苹果汁。 **Yì bēi píngguǒ zhī.** A glass of apple juice.

一	寸	扌	扎	执	执	热	热
热	热	热	热	热			

热

热 (Traditional)

rè　hot

灬 / 10 strokes

*The water is **hot**.*

热水　**rèshuǐ**　hot water
热狗　**règǒu**　hot dog
热情　**rèqíng**　enthusiastic, passionate
热身　**rèshēn**　warm up

Chinese Characters Writing Practice Pad—**Character #11**

你	要	什	么	？					
一	个	热	狗	。					

→ 你要什么？ **Nǐ yào shénme?** What do you want?

→ 一个热狗。 **Yí gè règǒu.** A hot dog.

丶	丷	丷	丷	兴	学	学	学
学	学	学					

学 學
Traditional

xué   to learn, to study
子 / 8 strokes

Learn to write your
letters neatly.

学生	**xuéshēng**	student
数学	**shùxué**	mathematics
学费	**xuéfèi**	tuition fee
学校	**xuéxiào**	school

Chinese Characters Writing Practice Pad—**Character #12**

你学什么？

数学。

→ 你学什么？ **Nǐ xué shénme?** What do you study?

→ 数学。 **Shùxué.** Mathematics.

么　么　么　么　么　么

么

麼
Traditional

me
丿 / 3 strokes

interrogative
particle; what

*"**What** did you say?"
asked the old man.*

什么	**shénme**	what
为什么	**wèishénme**	why
那么	**nàme**	in that case
多么	**duōme**	to what extent

Chinese Characters Writing Practice Pad—**Character #13**

这	是	什	么	？					
我	不	知	道	。					

→ 这是什么？ **Zhè shì shénme?** What is this?

→ 我不知道。 **Wǒ bù zhīdào.** I don't know.

二	土	土	耂	耂	者	者	者
都	都	都	都	都			

都

1. **dōu** all, both, entirely, (used for emphasis); even, already
2. **dū** capital city, metropolis

阝 / 10 strokes

*The **city** looks beautiful at night.*

全都	**quándōu**	all, without exception
都可以	**dōu kěyǐ**	all okay
都没有	**dōu méiyǒu**	none at all
首都	**shǒudū**	capital

Chinese Characters Writing Practice Pad—**Character #14**

你	要	吃	什	么	？				
什	么	都	可	以	。				

→ 你要吃什么？ **Nǐ yào chī shénme?**
What do you want to eat?

→ 什么都可以。 **Shénme dōu kěyǐ.** Anything is okay.

丨	╡	╡	北	北	北	北	北

北

běi   north

匕 / 5 strokes

*A compass always
points to the **north**.*

北方	**běifāng**	north
北京	**Běijīng**	Beijing
北欧	**Běi Ōu**	Northern Europe
东北	**dōngběi**	northeast

Chinese Characters Writing Practice Pad—**Character #15**

你去过北京吗？

还没有。

→ 你去过北京吗？ **Nǐ qù guò Běijīng ma?**
Have you been to Beijing?
→ 还没有。 **Hái méiyǒu.** Not yet.

| 丿 | 刁 | 水 | 水 | 水 | 水 | 水 |

水

shuǐ water

水 / 4 strokes

Water gushes from
the waterfall.

水果	**shuǐguǒ**	fruit
水瓶	**shuǐpíng**	water bottle
香水	**xiāngshuǐ**	perfume
开水	**kāishuǐ**	boiled water
水平	**shuǐpíng**	level, standard

Chinese Characters Writing Practice Pad—**Character #16**

你要喝什么？

有温开水吗？

→ 你要喝什么？ **Nǐ yào hē shénme?**
What do you want to drink?
→ 有温开水吗？ **Yǒu wēn kāishuǐ ma?**
Do you have warm water?

| 丿 | 仁 | 仁 | 午 | 午 | 午 | 午 | |

午

wǔ   noon

十 / 4 strokes

*It is **noon**, so the shadows are short.*

午餐	**wǔcān**	lunch, luncheon
午睡	**wǔshuì**	to take a nap
下午	**xiàwǔ**	afternoon
中午	**zhōngwǔ**	noon

Chinese Characters Writing Practice Pad—**Character #17**

什	么	时	候	有	空	？			
明	天	下	午	吧	。				

→ 什么时候有空？ **Shénme shíhou yǒu kòng?**
When are you free?

→ 明天下午吧。 **Míngtiān xiàwǔ ba.** Tomorrow afternoon.

| 一 | 二 | 于 | 开 | 开 | 开 | 开 | |

开　開
Traditional

kāi　to open

廾 / 4 strokes

*Please **open** the windows to let in some air.*

开放	**kāifàng**	to bloom, to open
开心	**kāixīn**	to feel happy; happy
公开	**gōngkāi**	to make public; public
打开	**dǎkāi**	to open

Chinese Characters Writing Practice Pad—**Character #18**

请	不	要	打	开	窗	户	。		
好	的	。							

→ 请不要打开窗户。 **Qǐng búyào dǎkāi chuānghu.**
Please don't open the window.

→ 好的。 **Hǎo de.** Sure.

九 九 九 九 九

九

jiǔ nine, 9
丿 / 2 strokes

九龍
→

*Kowloon means
"**nine** dragons."*

九月	**Jiǔyuè**	September
九龙	**Jiǔlóng**	Kowloon
十九	**shíjiǔ**	nineteen, 19
第九	**dì-jiǔ**	ninth

Chinese Characters Writing Practice Pad—**Character #19**

你 住 哪 儿 ？

我 住 九 龙 。

→ 你住哪儿？ **Nǐ zhù nǎr?** Where do you live?

→ 我住九龙。 **Wǒ zhù Jiǔlóng.** I live in Kowloon.

`	`	氵	汈	汉	汉	汉	汉

汉 漢
Traditional

hàn man

氵 / 5 strokes

*The **man** works hard,
planting rice.*

汉字	**Hànzì**	Chinese character
汉语	**Hànyǔ**	Chinese language
汉堡	**hànbǎo**	hamburger
好汉	**hǎohàn**	hero, courageous person

Chinese Characters Writing Practice Pad—**Character #20**

你最爱吃什么？

汉堡和薯条。

→ 你最爱吃什么？ **Nǐ zuì ài chī shénme?**
What do you like to eat most?

→ 汉堡和薯条。 **Hànbǎo hé shǔtiáo.** Hamburger and chips.

| 一 | 一 | 行 | 雨 | 雨 | 雨 | 雨 | 雨 |
| 雨 | 雨 | 雨 | | | | | |

雨

yǔ   rain

雨 / 8 strokes

*It is **raining** outside.*

雨天	**yǔtiān**	rainy day
雨伞	**yǔsǎn**	umbrella
雷雨	**léiyǔ**	thunderstorm
下雨	**xiàyǔ**	to rain

Chinese Characters Writing Practice Pad—**Character #21**

你带雨伞了吗？

没有。

→ 你带雨伞了吗？ **Nǐ dài yǔsǎn le ma?**
  Did you bring an umbrella?
→ 没有。 **Méiyǒu.** No.

一 十 土 圤 圤 坱 块 块

块 块

块
塊
Traditional

kuài
土 / 7 strokes

chunk; dollar; classifier
for pieces of cloth,
cake, soap etc.

*A big **piece** of
rock has fallen.*

一块	**yí kuài**	one block, one piece; one dollar
石块	**shíkuài**	stone, rock
冰块	**bīngkuài**	ice cube
鸡块	**jīkuài**	chicken nugget

Chinese Characters Writing Practice Pad—**Character #22**

请问你要什么？

三份鸡块。

→ 请问你要什么？ **Qǐngwèn nǐ yào shénme?**
What would you like?

→ 三份鸡块。 **Sān fèn jīkuài.**
Three portions of chicken nuggets.

没　　没　　没　　没　　没　　没　　没　　没

没　　没

没

méi　　have not, not

氵 / 7 strokes

"I have **no** money," said the boy.

没有	**méiyǒu**	do not have
没法	**méifǎ**	can't do anything
没用	**méiyòng**	useless
没关系	**méiguānxi**	no problem, it's OK

Chinese Characters Writing Practice Pad—**Character #23**

对不起。

没关系。

→ 对不起。 **Duìbuqǐ.** I am sorry.
→ 没关系。 **Méiguānxi.** No problem.

刁	又	对	对	对	对	对	对

对 對
Traditional

duì

寸 / 5 strokes

correct; pair; towards, at, for; to face

*Chopsticks always come in **pairs**.*

对话	**duìhuà**	dialogue
对了	**duìle**	correct, that's right
面对	**miànduì**	to face
派对	**pàiduì**	party (social)
一对	**yí duì**	a pair

Chinese Characters Writing Practice Pad—**Character #24**

对	不	对	？						
不	对	。							

→ 对不对？ **Duì búduì?** Correct?

→ 不对。 **Búduì!** Incorrect!

| 丿 | 儿 | 儿 | 儿 | 儿 | | |

儿　兒
Traditional

ér　child

儿 / 2 strokes

*The **child** is warmly wrapped up.*

儿女	**érnǚ**	children, sons and daughters
儿子	**érzi**	son
女儿	**nǚér**	daughter
一点儿	**yìdiǎnr**	a little, a bit

Chinese Characters Writing Practice Pad—**Character #25**

你有几个儿女？

我有两个女儿。

→ 你有几个儿女？ **Nǐ yǒu jǐ gè érnǚ?**
   How many children do you have?

→ 我有两个女儿。 **Wǒ yǒu liǎng gè nǚér.**
   I have two daughters.

㇒	㇕	口	艹	号	号	号	号

号 號
Traditional

hào number

口 / 5 strokes

*In some places 9 is considered
a lucky **number**.*

号码	**hàomǎ**	number
账号	**zhànghào**	account number
符号	**fúhào**	symbol
口号	**kǒuhào**	slogan
八号	**bā hào**	No. 8

Chinese Characters Writing Practice Pad—**Character #26**

你	的	电	话	号	码	是	多	少	？
九	二	三	四	五	六	七	八	。	

→ 你的电话号码是多少？ **Nǐ de diànhuà hàomǎ shì duōshao?**
What is your phone number?

→ 九二三四五六七八。 **Jiǔ èr sān sì wǔ liù qī bā.**
9234 5678.

| 𠂊 | 𠂤 | 𱼀 | 𱼁 | 饣 | 饭 | 饭 | 饭 |

| 饭 | 饭 | | | | | | |

饭　飯
Traditional

fàn　cooked rice, meal

饣 / 7 strokes

*I love curry chicken with **rice**.*

早饭	**zǎofàn**	breakfast
晚饭	**wǎnfàn**	evening meal
做饭	**zuòfàn**	to prepare a meal
稀饭	**xīfàn**	porridge

Chinese Characters Writing Practice Pad—**Character #27**

你 吃 过 早 饭 了 吗 ？

吃 过 了 。

→ 你吃过早饭了吗？ **Nǐ chī guò zǎofàn le ma?**
  Have you had your breakfast?
→ 吃过了。 **Chī guò le.** Yes, I did.

| 一 | 三 | 三 | 手 | 看 | 看 | 看 | 看 |

| 看 | 看 | 看 | 看 | | | | |

看

kàn   to see, to look

目 / 9 strokes

*My glasses help me **see** better.*

看到	**kàndào**	to see
看书	**kànshū**	to read
好看	**hǎokàn**	good-looking
难看	**nánkàn**	unsightly

Chinese Characters Writing Practice Pad—**Character #28**

这	件	裙	子	好	看	吗	？		
太	难	看	了	！					

→ 这件裙子好看吗？ **Zhè jiàn qúnzi hǎokàn ma?**
  Is this dress pretty?

→ 太难看了！ **Tài nánkàn le!** It's ugly!

ヲ 叉 叉' 叉ヶ 欢 欢 欢 欢

欢

欢
歡
Traditional

huān happy, welcome

欠 / 6 strokes

*A **happy** child!*

欢喜 **huānxǐ** happy
欢欢喜喜 **huānhuānxǐxǐ** happily
欢迎 **huānyíng** to welcome; welcome
喜欢 **xǐhuan** to like, be fond of

Chinese Characters Writing Practice Pad—**Character #29**

你喜欢猫吗？

不喜欢，我喜欢狗。

→ 你喜欢猫吗？ **Nǐ xǐhuan māo ma?** Do you like cats?

→ 不喜欢，我喜欢狗。 **Bú xǐhuan, wǒ xǐhuan gǒu.**
No, I like dogs.

多 | 夕 | 夕 | 多 | 多 | 多 | 多 | 多

多

duō   many, much

夕 / 6 strokes

*We don't have **much** oil.*

多少	**duōshao**	how much, how many?
许多	**xǔduō**	many, a lot of, much
太多	**tàiduō**	too much
更多	**gèngduō**	more, even more

Chinese Characters Writing Practice Pad—**Character #30**

十 个 苹 果 多 少 钱 ？

港 币 三 十 块 。

→ 十个苹果多少钱？ **Shí gè píngguǒ duōshao qián?**
How much for ten apples?

→ 港币三十块。 **Gǎng bì sānshí kuài.**
Thirty Hong Kong dollars.

` `	` ´ `	` ⸍ `	半	米	米	米	米
米							

米

mǐ　　rice, meter

米 / 6 strokes

*These cakes are made from **rice** flour.*

米饭	**mǐfàn**	cooked rice
厘米	**límǐ**	centimeter
纳米	**nàmǐ**	nanometer
糙米	**cāomǐ**	brown rice

Chinese Characters Writing Practice Pad—**Character #31**

我 爱 吃 糙 米 饭。

我 也 爱 吃。

→ 我爱吃糙米饭。 **Wǒ ài chī cāomǐfàn.**
 I love eating brown rice.
→ 我也爱吃。 **Wǒ yě ài chī.** Me too.

ㄱ 力 ﾟ力 边 边 边 边 边

边
邊
Traditional

biān   side, edge, margin

辶 / 5 strokes

The egg rolled to the edge of the table.

左边   **zuǒbiān**   left side
右边   **yòubiān**   right side
一边   **yì biān**   one side
边境   **biānjìng**   border

Chinese Characters Writing Practice Pad—**Character #32**

卫 生 间 在 哪 儿 ？

卫 生 间 在 左 边 。

→ 卫生间在哪儿？ **Wèishēngjiān zài nǎr?**
Where is the toilet?

→ 卫生间在左边。 **Wèishēngjiān zài zuǒbiān.**
The toilet is on the left.

一	ㄟ	丆	百	百	百	百	百
百							

百

bǎi
白 / 6 strokes

one hundred, numerous, many

*There are more than **one hundred** stars in the sky.*

百年	**bǎinián**	a hundred years
两百元	**liǎngbǎi yuán**	two hundred dollars
百分之五	**bǎifēnzhīwǔ**	five percent
百货商场	**bǎihuò shāngchǎng**	department store

Chinese Characters Writing Practice Pad—**Character #33**

这	件	红	裙	子	多	少	钱	?	
两	百	元	。						

→ 这件红裙子多少钱？ **Zhè jiàn hóng qúnzi duōshao qián?**
How much is this red dress?

→ 两百元。 **Liǎngbǎi yuán.** Two hundred dollars.

一 一 一 丐 亐 平 来 来 来

来 来

来 來
Traditional

lái to come, to arrive

木 / 7 strokes

*He **came** by car.*

回来	**huílái**	to return
来宾	**láibīn**	guest
来年	**láinián**	the coming year
未来	**wèilái**	future
来不及	**láibùjí**	not enough time

Chinese Characters Writing Practice Pad—**Character #34**

还	等	他	吗	?					
不	等	了	,	来	不	及	了	。	

→ 还等他吗？ **Hái děng tā ma?** Shall we wait for him?

→ 不等了，来不及了。 **Bùděngle, láibùjí le.**
No, there is not enough time.

一	十	才	木	杧	杯	杯	杯
杯	杯	杯					

杯

bēi　　glass, cup

木 / 8 strokes

We want two **glasses** *of beer.*

杯子	**bēizi**	cup, glass
纸杯	**zhǐbēi**	paper cup
干杯	**gānbēi**	to drink a toast, Cheers!
奖杯	**jiǎngbēi**	trophy cup

Chinese Characters Writing Practice Pad—**Character #35**

你家有酒杯吗？

没有，只有纸杯。

→ 你家有酒杯吗？ **Nǐ jiā yǒu jiǔbēi ma?**
Do you have wine glasses at home?

→ 没有，只有纸杯。 **Méiyǒu, zhǐyǒu zhǐbēi.**
No, only paper cups.

丬	ㅏ	上	占	占	占	点	点
点	点	点	点				

点
點
Traditional

diǎn   dot, point, drop

灬 / 9 strokes

Drops of rainwater
fell onto the glass.

点头	**diǎntóu**	to nod, to give the green light
点心	**diǎnxin**	dim sum, light refreshments
重点	**zhòngdiǎn**	main point, focus
缺点	**quēdiǎn**	weak point, shortcoming

Chinese Characters Writing Practice Pad—**Character #36**

午	饭	吃	什	么	？				
去	喝	茶	、		吃	点	心	，	好	吗
？									

→ 午饭吃什么？ **Wǔfàn chī shénme?**
What are we eating for lunch?

→ 去喝茶、吃点心，好吗？ **Qù hēchā, chī diǎnxin, hǎo ma?**
Let's go for tea and dimsum, shall we?

| 𠂉 | 𠂊 | 𠂋 | 𠂌 | 𠂍 | 𠂎 | 笃 | 笁 |

| 笁 | 笔 | 笔 | 笔 | 笔 | | | |

笔

筆
Traditional

*He writes with a **pen**.*

bǐ   pen, pencil

⺮⺮ / 10 strokes

铅笔	**qiānbǐ**	pencil
毛笔	**máobǐ**	writing brush
圆珠笔	**yuánzhūbǐ**	ball pen
笔记	**bǐjì**	notes
笔试	**bǐshì**	written test

Chinese Characters Writing Practice Pad—**Character #37**

我	想	买	一	支	自	动	铅	笔	。
十	块	。							

→ 我想买一支自动铅笔。 **Wǒ xiǎng mǎi yì zhī zìdòngqiānbǐ.**
I would like to buy a mechanical pencil.

→ 十块。 **Shí kuài.** Ten dollars.

`	``	`丷`	`⺍`	`前`	`前`	`前`	`前`
前	前	前	前				

前

qián front, forward, before

刂 / 9 strokes

*Alice is at the **front** of the queue.*

前面	**qiánmiàn**	in front
前天	**qiántiān**	the day before yesterday
以前	**yǐqián**	before, previous
向前	**xiàngqián**	forward, onward

Chinese Characters Writing Practice Pad—**Character #38**

厕所在哪儿？

前面，向前走一分钟。

→ 厕所在哪儿？ **Cèsuǒ zài nǎr?** Where is the toilet?

→ 前面，向前走一分钟。
Qiánmiàn, xiàng qián zǒu yì fēnzhōng.
It's in front, walk for a minute.

| J | 刂 | 小 | 小 | 小 | 小 | | |

小

xiǎo   small, tiny, few, young

小 / 3 strokes

*The plant has **tiny** shoots appearing.*

小姐	**xiǎojiě**	young lady, miss
小时	**xiǎoshí**	hour
小孩	**xiǎohái**	child
小心	**xiǎoxīn**	careful
很小	**hěn xiǎo**	very small

Chinese Characters Writing Practice Pad—**Character #39**

前	面	有	小	孩	，		小	心	！	
知	道	了	。							

→ 前面有小孩，小心！ **Qiánmiàn yǒu xiǎohái, xiǎoxīn!**
Children in front, be careful.

→ 知道了。 **Zhīdào le.** I will.

| 一 | 艹 | 艹 | 艹 | 艹 | 艹 | 艹 | 芸 |
| 芏 | 荦 | 菜 | 菜 | 菜 | 菜 | | |

菜

菜
Traditional

cài

艹 / 11 strokes

dish (type of food),
vegetable, cuisine

Vegetables are good
for our health.

菜单	**càidān**	menu
蔬菜	**shūcài**	vegetables
点菜	**diǎncài**	to order dishes
主菜	**zhǔcài**	main course
中国菜	**Zhōngguócài**	Chinese cuisine

Chinese Characters Writing Practice Pad—**Character #40**

有什么好吃的？

我们看菜单吧。

→ 有什么好吃的？ **Yǒu shénme hǎochī de?**
Anything good to eat?

→ 我们看菜单吧。 **Wǒmen kàn càidān ba.**
Let's read the menu.

| ⇃⇃ | 冂 | 日 | 日 | 日 | 日 | 日 | |

日

rì day

日 / 4 strokes

There are 28 **days**
in February.

节日	**jiérì**	festival
生日	**shēngrì**	birthday
日记	**rìjì**	diary
日常生活	**rìcháng shēnghuó**	daily life

Chinese Characters Writing Practice Pad—**Character #41**

你	送	他	什	么	生	日	礼	物	？
一	本	日	记	。					

→ 你送他什么生日礼物？ **Nǐ sòng tā shénme shēngrì lǐwù?**
What birthday present did you give him?

→ 一本日记。 **Yì běn rìjì.** A diary.

请 讠 讠 讠 讠 请 请 请

请 请 请 请 请

请

請
Traditional

qǐng

讠 / 10 strokes

to ask, to invite;
please (do sth)

Please sit down.

请问	**qǐngwèn**	excuse me, may I ask...?
请进	**qǐngjìn**	please come in
请假	**qǐngjià**	to apply for leave
请客	**qǐngkè**	to pay for the guests,
		to give a treat

Chinese Characters Writing Practice Pad—**Character #42**

请问陈老师在吗？

不在，他今天请假了。

→ 请问陈老师在吗？ **Qǐngwèn Chén lǎoshī zài ma?**
May I ask if Mr Chen is in?

→ 不在，他今天请假了。 **Búzài, tā jīntiān qǐngjià le.**
No, he's on leave today.

| ㇀ | 二 | 手 | 手 | 我 | 我 | 我 | 我 |
| 我 | 我 | | | | | | |

我

wǒ   I, me, my

戈 / 7 strokes

I have a twin sister.

我们	**wǒmen**	we, us
我的	**wǒde**	my, mine
自我	**zìwǒ**	self-
你我	**nǐwǒ**	you and I

Chinese Characters Writing Practice Pad—**Character #43**

你	可	以	帮	我	们	一	下	吗	？
可	以	。							

→ 你可以帮我们一下吗？ **Nǐ kěyǐ bāng wǒmen yíxià ma?**
Can you help us?

→ 可以。 **Kěyǐ.** Yes.

⼁	亻	亻	伫	住	住	住	住
住	住						

住

zhù

亻 / 7 strokes

to live, to reside,
to stop (sth)

*We **live** in the
countryside.*

住址	**zhùzhǐ**	address
住客	**zhùkè**	hotel guest, tenant
抓住	**zhuāzhù**	to grab, to capture
挡住	**dǎngzhù**	to obstruct

Chinese Characters Writing Practice Pad—**Character #44**

请 写 下 住 址。

好，我 住 北 京 路 一 号。

→ 请写下住址。 **Qǐng xiěxià zhùzhǐ.**
Please write down your address.

→ 好，我住北京路一号。 **Hǎo, wǒ zhù Běijīng Lù yī hào.**
Ok. I live at No.1 Beijing Road.

⌇	口	口	叮	叼	叼	呀	哪
哪	哪	哪	哪				

哪

nǎ   how, which, where

口 / 9 strokes

*The sign shows you **where** the restrooms are.*

哪个	**nǎge**	which one?
哪些	**nǎxiē**	which ones?
哪儿	**nǎr**	where?
天哪	**tiānna**	good gracious!

Chinese Characters Writing Practice Pad—**Character #45**

你去过哪些国家？

我只去过中国和美国。

→ 你去过哪些国家？ **Nǐ qù guò nǎxiē guójiā?**
Which countries have you been to?

→ 我只去过中国和美国。 **Wǒ zhǐ qù guò Zhōngguó hé Měiguó.** I have only been to China and the United States.

`	亻	白	白	白	的	的	的
的	的	的					

的

1. **de**　　of, ~'s (possessive particle)
2. **dì**　　purpose

白 / 8 strokes

Name: Bob Taylor

This is Bob's book.

我的	**wǒde**	my, mine
是的	**shìde**	yes, that's right
目的	**mùdì**	purpose, aim
目的地	**mùdìdì**	destination

Chinese Characters Writing Practice Pad—**Character #46**

他 吃 了 我 的 饼 干 吗 ？

是 的 。

→ 他吃了我的饼干吗？ **Tā chī le wǒde bǐnggān ma?**
Did he eat my biscuits?
→ 是的。 **Shìde.** Yes, he did.

一	艹	艹	艻	芡	苓	芩	荼
茶	茶	茶	茶				

茶

chá　　tea, tea plant

艹 / 9 strokes

*We love **tea**, especially English tea.*

茶叶	**cháyè**	tea, tea leaves
茶杯	**chábēi**	tea cup, glass, mug
绿茶	**lùchá**	green tea
奶茶	**nǎichá**	milk tea

Chinese Characters Writing Practice Pad—**Character #47**

你 喝 绿 茶 还 是 奶 茶 ?

奶 茶 。

→ 你喝绿茶还是奶茶？ **Nǐ hē lùchá háishi nǎichá?**
  Do you want green tea or milk tea?

→ 奶茶。**Nǎichá.** Milk tea.

名

míng

口 / 6 strokes

name, position (as among competitors); famous; classifier for people

*This is the statue of a **famous** person.*

名字	**míngzi**	name
名人	**míngrén**	celebrity
有名	**yǒumíng**	famous, well-known
报名	**bàomíng**	to apply, to register; application

Chinese Characters Writing Practice Pad—**Character #48**

学 日 文 吗 ?

我 报 名 了 。

→ 学日文吗？ **Xué Rìwén ma?** Learning Japanese?

→ 我报名了。 **Wǒ bàomíng le.** I have enrolled.

丨	冂	冂	同	同	同	同	同
同							

同

tóng

口 / 6 strokes

same; together, alike, with

*The cup comes **together** with this saucer.*

同学	**tóngxué**	classmate
同事	**tóngshì**	colleague
同意	**tóngyì**	to agree; agreement
不同	**bùtóng**	different

Chinese Characters Writing Practice Pad—**Character #49**

你	同	意	吗	？					
不	同	意	。						

→ 你同意吗？ **Nǐ tóngyì ma?** Do you agree?

→ 不同意。 **Bù tóngyì.** No, I disagree.

说 说 说 说 说 说 说 说

说 说 说 说

说 說
Traditional

shuō to speak, to say,
讠 / 9 strokes to explain

*This book **explains**
English grammar.*

说话	**shuōhuà**	to speak
说明	**shuōmíng**	to explain, to illustrate
说服	**shuōfú**	to persuade, to convince
小说	**xiǎoshuō**	novel, fiction

Chinese Characters Writing Practice Pad—**Character #50**

你的弟弟会说话吗？

会，他已经三岁了。

→ 你的弟弟会说话吗？ **Nǐ de dìdi huì shuōhuà ma?**
Can your younger brother talk?

→ 会，他已经三岁了。 **Huì, tā yǐjīng sān suì le.**
Yes, he's already three.

| 一 | 丆 | 石 | 而 | 而 | 而 | 面 |
| 面 | 面 | 面 | 面 | | | |

面

麵 (flour/noodle)
Traditional

I love eating cold **noodles** in summer.

miàn

面 / 9 strokes

flour, noodles, side

面包	**miànbāo**	bread, bun
拉面	**lāmiàn**	ramen, noodles
后面	**hòumiàn**	back, rear
前面	**qiánmiàn**	front

Chinese Characters Writing Practice Pad—**Character #51**

我	爱	吃	牛	肉	拉	面	。		
前	面	就	有	一	家	拉	面	店	。

→ 我爱吃牛肉拉面。 **Wǒ ài chī niúròu lāmiàn.**
I like to eat beef ramen.

→ 前面就有一家拉面店。 **Qiánmiàn jiù yǒu yì jiā lāmiàn diàn.** There is a ramen noodle shop not far from here.

中 | 冖 | 口 | 中 | 中 | 中 | 中

中

zhōng   middle, center;
丨 / 4 strokes   while (doing sth)

*My father is the **middle** person in that photo.*

中间   **zhōngjiān**   middle
中秋节   **Zhōngqiūjié**   Mid-Autumn Festival
中文   **Zhōngwén**   Chinese language
中心   **zhōngxīn**   center

Chinese Characters Writing Practice Pad—**Character #52**

你会中文吗？

会一点儿。

→ 你会中文吗？ **Nǐ huì Zhōngwén ma?**
Do you know Chinese?

→ 会一点儿。 **Huì yìdiǎnr.** A little bit.

什　　　　　什　　什　　什

什

甚
Traditional

shén　what

亻 / 4 strokes

What fruit is this? I have not seen it before.

什么	**shénme**	What?
为什么	**wèishénme**	Why?
什么事	**shénme shì**	What's the matter?
什么人	**shénme rén**	Who?

Chinese Characters Writing Practice Pad—**Character #53**

你 在 干 什 么 ？

看 书 。

→ 你在干什么？ **Nǐ zài gàn shénme?** What are you doing?
→ 看书。 **Kàn shū.** Reading a book.

| 一 | ナ | 方 | 友 | 友 | 友 | 友 | |

友

yǒu   friend

又 / 4 strokes

*Emily is my best **friend**.*

友谊	**yǒuyì**	friendship
朋友	**péngyou**	friend
友善	**yǒushàn**	friendly
交友	**jiāoyǒu**	to make friends

Chinese Characters Writing Practice Pad—**Character #54**

交友要小心。

知道了。

→ 交友要小心。 **Jiāo yǒu yào xiǎoxīn.**
You have to be careful when making friends.
→ 知道了。 **Zhīdào le.** I know.

| 一 | 十 | 才 | 木 | 村 | 相 | 相 | 相 |
| 相 | 相 | 想 | 想 | 想 | 想 | 想 | 想 |

想

xiǎng

心 / 13 strokes

to think, to believe, to want

*I **want** to have an ice cream.*

想法	**xiǎngfǎ**	idea, opinion
想起	**xiǎngqǐ**	to think of
梦想	**mèngxiǎng**	to dream of; dream
感想	**gǎnxiǎng**	reflections, thoughts

Chinese Characters Writing Practice Pad—**Character #55**

你 有 什 么 想 法 吗 ?

没 有 。

→ 你有什么想法吗？ **Nǐ yǒu shénme xiǎngfǎ ma?**
Do you have any opinion?

→ 没有。 **Méiyǒu.** No.

| 亻 | 彳 | 彳 | 彳 | 彳 | 彳 | 很 | 很 |
| 很 | 很 | 很 | 很 | | | | |

很

hěn   very

彳 / 9 strokes

*Sumos are **very** big.*

很多	**hěn duō**	very many, a lot
很快	**hěn kuài**	very quick
很少	**hěn shǎo**	seldom; few
很好	**hěn hǎo**	very good

Chinese Characters Writing Practice Pad—**Character #56**

吃光了？

你炒的鸡蛋很好吃。

→ 吃光了？ **Chīguāng le?** Finished eating everything?

→ 你炒的鸡蛋很好吃。 **Nǐ chǎo de jīdàn hěn hǎochī.**
Your fried egg is very tasty.

╱	㇏	ㅅ⸴	ㅅㅅ	ㅅㅅ⟶	坐	坐⟶	坐
坐	坐						

坐

zuò   to sit, to take a seat

土 / 7 strokes

*The little child **sits** quietly in his chair.*

坐飞机	**zuò fēijī**	to take an airplane
坐火车	**zuò huǒchē**	to take a train
坐巴士	**zuò bāshì**	to take a bus
让坐	**ràngzuò**	to give up a seat

Chinese Characters Writing Practice Pad—**Character #57**

坐	火	车	好	吗	?				
坐	巴	士	比	较	方	便	。		

→ 坐火车好吗？ **Zuò huǒchē hǎo ma?** Shall we take a train?

→ 坐巴士比较方便。 **Zuò bāshì bǐjiào fāngbiàn.**
Taking a bus is more convenient.

生　乍　乍　牛　生　生　生　生

生

shēng to give birth;
生 / 5 strokes　life, student

*He is a primary school **student**.*

生肖　　**shēngxiào**　animals according to the
　　　　　　　　　　　Chinese zodiac
生活　　**shēnghuó**　to live; livelihood
生病　　**shēngbìng**　to fall ill
花生　　**huāshēng**　peanuts

Chinese Characters Writing Practice Pad—**Character #58**

小	张	为	什	么	没	有	上	班	？
他	又	生	病	了	。				

→ 小张为什么没有上班？ **Xiǎo Zhāng wèishénme méiyǒu shàngbān?** Why hasn't Xiaozhang come to work?

→ 他又生病了。 **Tā yòu shēngbìng le.** He has fallen ill again.

一	力	才	右	在	在	在	在
在							

在

zài　　at, in

土 / 6 strokes

*Look! There are two chicks **in** the basket.*

在线　　**zàixiàn**　　online
现在　　**xiànzài**　　now, at present
存在　　**cúnzài**　　to exist; existence
正在　　**zhèngzài**　　in the middle of doing
　　　　　　　　　　　　something

Chinese Characters Writing Practice Pad—**Character #59**

你现在有空吗？

没有，我正在做饭。

→ 你现在有空吗？ **Nǐ xiànzài yǒu kòng ma?**
   Do you have time now?
→ 没有，我正在做饭。 **Méiyǒu, wǒ zhèngzài zuòfàn.**
   No, I am preparing a meal.

㇅	㇅	㇅	三	买	买	买	买
买							

买　　　買
　　　　Traditional

mǎi　　to buy, to purchase

乙 / 6 strokes

*I want to **buy** roses for my mom.*

买卖	**mǎimài**	buying and selling
买家	**mǎijiā**	buyer, client
买票	**mǎipiào**	to buy tickets
购买	**gòumǎi**	to buy

Chinese Characters Writing Practice Pad—**Character #60**

在 哪 儿 买 火 车 票 ？

你 可 以 到 网 上 买 。

→ 在哪儿买火车票？ **Zài nǎr mǎi huǒchēpiào?**
Where do I buy a train ticket?

→ 你可以到网上买。 **Nǐ kěyǐ dào wǎngshàng mǎi.**
You can buy it online.

| 习 | 习 | 习 | 习 | 习 | 习 | | |

习
習
Traditional

She loves to **practice** singing aloud.

xí
乙 / 3 strokes

to practice,
to be used to

练习   **liànxí**   to practice; practice
习惯   **xíguàn**   habit
学习   **xuéxí**   to learn, to study
复习   **fùxí**   to revise; revision

Chinese Characters Writing Practice Pad—**Character #61**

我	的	中	文	不	好	。			
多	练	习	,		就	会	有	进	步	。

→ 我的中文不好。 **Wǒ de Zhōngwén bùhǎo.**
My Chinese is not good.

→ 多练习，就会有进步。 **Duō liànxí, jiù huì yǒu jìnbù.**
Practice more and you will improve.

丨	冂	冂	冋	回	回	回	回
回							

回

huí   to return

口 / 6 strokes

*Please **return** your books by tomorrow.*

回答	**huídá**	to reply; reply
回来	**huílái**	to return
回家	**huíjiā**	to return home
来回	**láihuí**	to and fro

Chinese Characters Writing Practice Pad—**Character #62**

晚	上	十	点	去	喝	咖	啡	?	
太	晚	了	！	该	回	家	了	！	

→ 晚上十点去喝咖啡？ **Wǎnshàng shí diǎn qù hē kāfēi?**
Come out for coffee at ten tonight?

→ 太晚了！该回家了！ **Tài wǎn le! Gāi huíjiā le!**
Too late! It is time to go home.

乀	八	少	父	父	爷	爸	爸
爸	爸	爸					

爸

bà father, dad

父 / 8 strokes

*My **dad** is a doctor.*

爸爸	**bàba**	father
爸妈	**bàmā**	dad and mom
老爸	**lǎobà**	old dad (colloq.)
兔爸	**tùbà**	toolbar (loanword)

Chinese Characters Writing Practice Pad—**Character #63**

你	们	给	爸	爸	买	什	么	礼	物
？									
我	们	买	了	一	部	手	机	。	

→ 你们给爸爸买什么礼物？ **Nǐmen gěi bàba mǎi shénme lǐwù?** What present are you giving your dad?

→ 我们买了一部手机。 **Wǒmen mǎi le yí bù shǒujī.** We bought a mobile phone.

一	冇	丂	丂	歹	歹	医	医
医	医						

医

醫
Traditional

yī
匚 / 7 strokes

medical; medicine,
doctor; to cure, to treat

Please take this **medicine** *for your cough.*

医院	**yīyuàn**	hospital
医生	**yīshēng**	doctor
牙医	**yáyī**	dentist
名医	**míngyī**	famous doctor

Chinese Characters Writing Practice Pad—**Character #64**

请问医院在哪儿？

一直走，到路口左转。

→ 请问医院在哪儿？ **Qǐngwèn yīyuàn zài nǎr?**
May I ask, where is the hospital?

→ 一直走，到路口左转。 **Yìzhí zǒu, dào lùkǒu zuǒ zhuǎn.**
Go straight, turn left at the junction.

| ㇇ | 了 | 子 | 子 | 子 | 子 | | |

子

zǐ

子 / 3 strokes

son, child, seed, egg, small thing

This plant grows from a tiny **seed**.

妻子	**qīzi**	wife
孩子	**háizi**	children
句子	**jùzi**	sentence
瓶子	**píngzi**	bottle
筷子	**kuàizi**	chopsticks

Chinese Characters Writing Practice Pad—**Character #65**

你 有 几 个 孩 子 ？

三 个 。

→ 你有几个孩子？ **Nǐ yǒu jǐ gè háizi?**
How many children do you have?

→ 三个。 **Sān gè.** Three.

个

个 个 个 个 个 个

个 個
Traditional

gè
人 / 3 strokes

individual; general
classifier for things

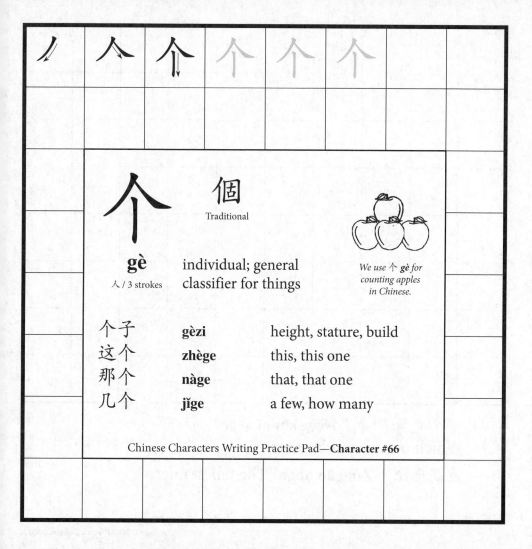

We use 个 gè for counting apples in Chinese.

个子　　**gèzi**　　height, stature, build
这个　　**zhège**　　this, this one
那个　　**nàge**　　that, that one
几个　　**jǐge**　　a few, how many

Chinese Characters Writing Practice Pad—**Character #66**

哪 个 是 你 哥 哥 ?

最 高 那 个 。

→ 哪个是你哥哥？ **Nǎge shì nǐ gēge?**
Which one is your brother?

→ 最高那个。 **Zuì gāo nàge.** The tallest one.

上 ｜ ▶ 上 上 上 上

上

shàng up

一 / 3 strokes

*Look **up**! There is something on the ceiling.*

上网	**shàngwǎng**	to go online
上午	**shàngwǔ**	morning
上课	**shàngkè**	to go to class
上班	**shàngbān**	to go to work

Chinese Characters Writing Practice Pad—**Character #67**

你	星	期	六	做	什	么	？		
我	喜	欢	到	网	吧	上	网	。	

→ 你星期六做什么？ **Nǐ Xīngqīliù zuò shénme?**
What are you doing on Saturday?

→ 我喜欢到网吧上网。 **Wǒ xǐhuan dào wǎngbā shàngwǎng.**
I like to go online in the Internet cafe.

| 阝 | 阝 | 阝 | 阝 | 阸 | 阹 | 陀 | 院 |
| 院 | 院 | 院 | 院 | | | | |

院

yuàn

阝 / 9 strokes

courtyard, institution

*My bike is in the **courtyard**.*

院子	**yuànzi**	courtyard
法院	**fǎyuàn**	court of law
医学院	**yīxuéyuàn**	medical school
电影院	**diànyǐngyuàn**	cinema

Chinese Characters Writing Practice Pad—**Character #68**

你 在 哪 个 大 学 ？

我 在 北 京 医 学 院 。

→ 你在哪个大学？ **Nǐ zài nǎge dàxué?**
Which university do you go to?

→ 我在北京医学院。 **Wǒ zài Běijīng Yīxuéyuàn.**
I go to Beijing Medical College.

| 丨 | 冂 | 冈 | 四 | 四 | 四 | 四 | 四 |

四

sì   four

口 / 5 strokes

Four birds chirping away merrily.

四个星期	**sì gè xīngqī**	four weeks
四季	**sìjì**	four seasons
四十	**sìshí**	forty
十四	**shísì**	fourteen

Chinese Characters Writing Practice Pad—**Character #69**

一年四季，我最喜欢秋
季。

我怕冷，夏天最好。

→ 一年四季，我最喜欢秋季。 **Yì nián sìjì, wǒ zuì xǐhuan qiūjì.** Of the four seasons, I like autumn most.

→ 我怕冷，夏天最好。 **Wǒ pà lěng, xiàtiān zuìhǎo.** I can't stand the cold, summer is the best.

| 丶 | 亠 | 亠 | 高 | 亠 | 亠 | 高 | 高 |

| 高 | 高 | 高 | 高 | 高 | | | |

高

gāo   high, tall

高 / 10 strokes

*This pole is very **high**.*

高级   **gāojí**   high level, advanced
高兴   **gāoxìng**   happy
高山   **gāoshān**   high mountain
提高   **tígāo**   to increase, to raise

Chinese Characters Writing Practice Pad—**Character #70**

怎	样	提	高	中	文	水	平	？	
多	听	多	说	多	看	书	吧	。	

→ 怎样提高中文水平？ **Zěnyàng tígāo Zhōngwén shuǐpíng?**
How do I improve my Chinese?

→ 多听多说多看书吧。 **Duō tīng duō shuō duō kàn shū ba.**
Listen, speak and read more.

話

丶	讠	讠	讠	讠	讠	话	话
话	话	话					

话

話
Traditional

huà
讠 / 8 strokes

speech, talk,
language, dialect

*My son **talks** to my
mom every day.*

话剧	**huàjù**	stage play, drama
笑话	**xiàohuà**	joke
假话	**jiǎhuà**	lies
废话	**fèihuà**	nonsense

Chinese Characters Writing Practice Pad—**Character #71**

他 总 是 说 假 话。

是 吗? 我 还 相 信 他 啦!

→ 他总是说假话。 **Tā zǒngshì shuō jiǎhuà.**
He keeps telling lies.

→ 是吗? 我还相信他啦! **Shì ma? Wǒ hái xiāngxìn tā la!**
Really? I believed all he said.

气　气　气　气　气　气　气

气

氣
Traditional

qì　　gas, air, weather
气 / 4 strokes

*What lovely **weather**! I can go for a stroll.*

空气　　**kōngqì**　　air
天气　　**tiānqì**　　weather
气球　　**qìqiú**　　balloon
生气　　**shēngqì**　　angry; to take offense

Chinese Characters Writing Practice Pad—**Character #72**

你	为	什	么	不	说	话	？		
我	很	生	气	。					

→ 你为什么不说话？ **Nǐ wèishénme bù shuōhuà?**
Why aren't you saying anything?

→ 我很生气。 **Wǒ hěn shēngqì.** I am angry.

ㄱ 马 书 书 书 书 书

书 書
Traditional

shū book

一 / 4 strokes

*I copy recipes into this **book**.*

书店   **shūdiàn**   bookstore
脸书   **Liǎnshū**   Facebook
秘书   **mìshū**   secretary
图书馆   **túshūguǎn**   library

Chinese Characters Writing Practice Pad—**Character #73**

喜	欢	你	脸	书	上	的	照	片	。
我	在	日	本	拍	的	。			

→ 喜欢你脸书上的照片。 **Xǐhuan nǐ Liǎnshū shàng de zhàopiàn.** I like the photos on your Facebook.

→ 我在日本拍的。 **Wǒ zài Rìběn pāi de.**
I took them in Japan.

| 刂 | 冂 | 刃 | 见 | 见 | 见 | 见 | |

见　見
Traditional

jiàn　　to see, to meet

见 / 4 strokes

*It is nice **to meet** old friends again.*

见面	**jiànmiàn**	to meet face to face; meeting
再见	**zàijiàn**	see you again, goodbye
意见	**yìjiàn**	opinion, viewpoint
看见	**kànjiàn**	to see

Chinese Characters Writing Practice Pad—**Character #74**

你	有	什	么	意	见	？			
明	天	见	面	再	说	吧	。		

→ 你有什么意见？ **Nǐ yǒu shénme yìjiàn?**
What's your opinion?

→ 明天见面再说吧。 **Míngtiān jiànmiàn zài shuō ba.**
Let's talk when we meet tomorrow.

视

视
Traditional

shì

衤 / 8 strokes

to look at,
to inspect

*To inspect the
plant for worms*

视力   **shìlì**   vision, eyesight
电视   **diànshì**   television
近视   **jìnshì**   shortsighted, myopia
忽视   **hūshì**   to neglect, to ignore

Chinese Characters Writing Practice Pad—**Character #75**

我 的 近 视 加 深 了 。

你 要 少 看 电 视 了 。

→ 我的近视加深了。 **Wǒ de jìnshì jiāshēn le.**
My shortsightedness has increased.

→ 你要少看电视了。 **Nǐ yào shǎo kàn diànshì le.**
You have to watch less television.

⺍	⺍⺋	⺍⺋	⺍⺋	⺍⺋	兴	兴	觉
觉	觉	觉	觉				

觉 覺
Traditional

He took *a nap* after lunch.

1. **jué**   to feel, to be aware
2. **jiào**   a nap, sleep

见 / 9 strokes

自觉	**zìjué**	consciousness, self-awareness
发觉	**fājué**	to feel, to discover
听觉	**tīngjué**	sense of hearing
睡觉	**shuìjiào**	to sleep

Chinese Characters Writing Practice Pad—**Character #76**

我 每 天 睡 十 个 小 时 。

睡 觉 是 最 好 的 享 受 。

→ 我每天睡十个小时。 **Wǒ měitiān shuì shí gè xiǎoshí.**
  I sleep 10 hours every day.

→ 睡觉是最好的享受。 **Shuìjiào shì zuìhǎo de xiǎngshòu.**
  Sleeping is the best enjoyment.

二

èr   two, 2

二 / 2 strokes

*It takes **two** hands to clap.*

二手	**èrshǒu**	second-hand
二十	**èrshí**	twenty, 20
二月	**Éryuè**	February
第二	**dì-èr**	second

Chinese Characters Writing Practice Pad—**Character #77**

你	的	车	子	很	漂	亮	。		
是	吗	？	是	二	手	车	。		

→ 你的车子很漂亮。 **Nǐ de chēzi hěn piàoliang.**
Your car is very nice.

→ 是吗？是二手车。 **Shì ma? Shì èrshǒuchē.**
Really? It's a second-hand car.

五

wǔ   five, 5

二 / 4 strokes

Five fingers on one hand

五月	**Wǔyuè**	May
五十	**wǔshí**	fifty, 50
十五	**shíwǔ**	fifteen, 15
五花八门	**wǔhuā-bāmén**	of a wide variety, all kinds of, myriad

Chinese Characters Writing Practice Pad—**Character #78**

端午节我们吃粽子。

妈妈做了五十个粽子。

→ 端午节我们吃粽子。 **Duānwǔjié wǒmen chī zòngzi.**
We eat dumplings during the Dragon Boat Festival.

→ 妈妈做了五十个粽子。 **Māma zuò le wǔshí gè zòngzi.**
Mum made fifty dumplings.

⺊	⺊	⺊⺊	止	止	此	些	些
些	些	些					

些

xiē   some, few

二 / 8 strokes

*Here are **some** sweets for you.*

这些	**zhèxiē**	these
一些	**yìxiē**	some, a few
那些	**nàxiē**	those
哪些	**nǎxiē**	which ones?

Chinese Characters Writing Practice Pad—**Character #79**

哪些国家不用签证？

这些国家不用签证。

→ 哪些国家不用签证？ **Nǎxiē guójiā búyòng qiānzhèng?**
   Which countries don't require visas?
→ 这些国家不用签证。 **Zhèxiē guójiā búyòng qiānzhèng.**
   These countries don't require visas.

丿	冂	冃	甩	电	电	电	电

电

電
Traditional

diàn   electric; electricity

田 / 5 strokes

*This is an **electric** bulb.*

电话　　**diànhuà**　　　telephone, telephone call
电脑　　**diànnǎo**　　　computer
电梯　　**diàntī**　　　　elevator
电子邮件　**diànzǐyóujiàn**　email

Chinese Characters Writing Practice Pad—**Character #80**

你 为 什 么 没 有 来 开 会 ？

我 的 电 脑 坏 了 。

→ 你为什么没有来开会？ **Nǐ wèishénme méiyǒu lái kāihuì?**
Why didn't you come for the meeting?

→ 我的电脑坏了。 **Wǒ de diànnǎo huài le.**
My computer broke down.

| 丷 | 日 | 日 | 日 | 日 | 昙 | 昙 | 景 |

| 景 | 景 | 景 | 景 | 影 | 影 | 影 | 影 |

影

yǐng

彡 / 15 strokes

picture, image, film, movie, shadow; to take a photo

*The light casts a **shadow** onto the wall.*

电影	**diànyǐng**	movie, film
影响	**yǐngxiǎng**	to affect; influence
影子	**yǐngzi**	shadow
摄影	**shèyǐng**	photography

Chinese Characters Writing Practice Pad—**Character #81**

我	喜	欢	晚	上	看	电	影	。	
这	会	影	响	你	的	健	康	。	

→ 我喜欢晚上看电影。 **Wǒ xǐhuan wǎnshàng kàn diànyǐng.**
 I like watching movies at night.

→ 这会影响你的健康。 **Zhè huì yǐngxiǎng nǐ de jiànkāng.**
 It will affect your health.

一	十	才	木	术	朾	朾	校
栌	校	校	校	校			

校

xiào   school,
木 / 10 strokes   military officer

*This is my **school**.*
I love being here.

校长	**xiàozhǎng**	headmaster, principal
校园	**xiàoyuán**	campus
校服	**xiàofú**	school uniform
校舍	**xiàoshè**	school campus

Chinese Characters Writing Practice Pad—**Character #82**

这	个	校	园	很	大	。			
听	说	校	服	也	很	漂	亮	。	

→ 这个校园很大。 **Zhège xiàoyuán hěn dà.**
This campus is big.

→ 听说校服也很漂亮。 **Tīngshuō xiàofú yě hěn piàoliang.**
I heard that the school uniform is also beautiful.

`	丷	宀	宀	宀	客	客	客
客	客	客	客				

客

kè   customer, visitor, guest

宀 / 9 strokes

*This **visitor** has a carton of gifts for the school.*

客人	**kèrén**	visitor, guest
博客	**bókè**	blogger
黑客	**hēikè**	hacker
乘客	**chéngkè**	passenger

Chinese Characters Writing Practice Pad—**Character #83**

客人到了。

请客人在外面等一等。

→ 客人到了。 **Kèrén dào le.** The guest is here.

→ 请客人在外面等一等。 **Qǐng kèrén zài wàimiàn děngyìděng.** Please ask the guest to wait outside for a while.

丶	丷	宀	宁	宁	宁	家	家
家	家	家	家	家			

家

jiā   home, family

宀 / 10 strokes

Home is where one's beloved ones are.

家庭	**jiātíng**	family, household
家乡	**jiāxiāng**	hometown
家人	**jiārén**	family member
回家	**huíjiā**	to return home

Chinese Characters Writing Practice Pad—**Character #84**

我 和 家 人 见 面 的 时 间 不
多 。

因 为 你 每 天 很 晚 才 回 家
。

→ 我和家人见面的时间不多。 **Wǒ hé jiārén jiànmiàn de shí-jiān bù duō.** I don't have much time to see my family members.

→ 因为你每天很晚才回家。 **Yīnwèi nǐ měitiān hěn wǎn cái huíjiā.** It's because you go home very late every night.

卜	卜	占	占	占	占	卓	卓

桌	桌	桌	桌	桌			

桌

zhuō   table, desk

木 / 10 strokes

*This is my study **desk**.*

桌面	**zhuōmiàn**	desktop, tabletop
桌子	**zhuōzi**	table, desk
桌球	**zhuōqiú**	billiards, snooker
餐桌	**cānzhuō**	dining table

Chinese Characters Writing Practice Pad—**Character #85**

这张照片很美。

给你，放在你的桌面。

→ 这张照片很美。 **Zhè zhāng zhàopiàn hěn měi.**
This photo is very pretty.

→ 给你，放在你的桌面。 **Gěi nǐ, fàng zài nǐ de zhuōmiàn.**
A present for you to put on your desktop.

ニ	十	士	去	去	去	去	去

去

qù　　to go, to remove

厶 / 5 strokes

*This will **remove** the stains from my clothes.*

上去	**shàngqù**	to go up
过去	**guòqù**	(in the) past
失去	**shīqù**	to lose
回去	**huíqù**	to go back
去世	**qùshì**	to pass away (formal)

Chinese Characters Writing Practice Pad—**Character #86**

什 么 时 候 去 美 国 ?

下 个 星 期 。

→ 什么时候去美国？ **Shénme shíhou qù Měiguó?**
  When are you going to the States?

→ 下个星期。 **Xià gè xīngqī.** Next week.

人　人　人　人　人

人

rén　　man, person, people

人 / 2 strokes

*That **person** walks very fast.*

人民　　**rénmín**　　the people
人口　　**rénkǒu**　　population
成人　　**chéngrén**　　adult
别人　　**biérén**　　other people

Chinese Characters Writing Practice Pad—**Character #87**

我 没 错。

不 要 老 是 责 怪 别 人。

→ 我没错。 **Wǒ méi cuò.** Not my fault.

→ 不要老是责怪别人。 **Búyào lǎoshì zéguài biérén.**
Don't always blame others.

| 亻 | 人 | 仒 | 今 | 今 | 今 | 今 | |

今

jīn

人 / 4 strokes

the present, this, now

*The cat is **now** sleeping.*

今天	**jīntiān**	today
今年	**jīnnián**	this year
今后	**jīnhòu**	from now on
当今	**dāngjīn**	present, now

Chinese Characters Writing Practice Pad—**Character #88**

我 考 试 不 合 格 ！

今 后 要 更 加 努 力 。

→ 我考试不合格！ **Wǒ kǎoshì bù hégé!**
I failed my examination.
→ 今后要更加努力。 **Jīnhòu yào gèngjiā nǔlì.**
From now on, you have to work harder.

↓	口	曰	叩	叫↓	叫	叫	叫

叫

jiào   to call, be named

口 / 5 strokes

COME HERE!!

"Come here!" called his mom.

叫好	**jiàohǎo**	to applaud, to cheer
大叫	**dàjiào**	to shout
叫醒	**jiàoxǐng**	to wake somebody up
名叫	**míngjiào**	called, named

Chinese Characters Writing Practice Pad—**Character #89**

明天早点叫醒我。

好，我在你耳边大叫！

→ 明天早点叫醒我。 **Míngtiān zǎodiǎn jiàoxǐng wǒ.**
Wake me up earlier tomorrow.

→ 好, 我在你耳边大叫！ **Hǎo, wǒ zài nǐ ěrbiān dà jiào!**
Ok, I'll shout in your ear.

⼀	十	才	木	朮	朾	样	样
样	样	样	样	样			

样
様
Traditional

yàng
木 / 10 strokes

manner, pattern,
way, appearance

*This dress has
many **patterns**.*

样子	**yàngzi**	appearance
各样	**gèyàng**	different types
一样	**yīyàng**	same
样品	**yàngpǐn**	sample

Chinese Characters Writing Practice Pad—**Character #90**

到	哪	里	买	东	西	最	好	？	
超	市	有	各	式	各	样	货	品	。

→ 到哪里买东西最好？ **Dào nǎli mǎi dōngxi zuìhǎo?**
Where is the best place to shop?

→ 超市有各式各样货品。 **Chāoshì yǒu gèshì-gèyàng huòpǐn.**
There are all kinds of goods in a supermarket.

他

他

tā he or him, other, another

亻 / 5 strokes

He wears a striped tie today.

他们   **tāmen**   they
他人   **tārén**   other people
其他   **qítā**   other, the rest
吉他   **jítā**   guitar (loanword)

Chinese Characters Writing Practice Pad—**Character #91**

为 什 么 女 生 都 喜 欢 他 ？

他 太 牛 了 。

→ 为什么女生都喜欢他？ **Wèishénme nǚshēng dōu xǐhuan tā?** Why do the girls like him?

→ 他太牛了。 **Tā tài niú le.** He's awesome.

亻	亻	亻	们	们	们	们	们

们

門
Traditional

men
亻 / 5 strokes

plural marker for pronouns, and nouns referring to individuals

They enter the house through the front door.

我们	**wǒmen**	we, us, our
你们	**nǐmen**	you (plural)
他们	**tāmen**	they
人们	**rénmen**	people
学生们	**xuéshēngmen**	students

Chinese Characters Writing Practice Pad—**Character #92**

| 你 | 们 | 中 | 午 | 吃 | 了 | 什 | 么 | ? | |
| 我 | 们 | 吃 | 了 | 自 | 助 | 餐 | 。 | | |

→ 你们中午吃了什么？ **Nǐmen zhōngwǔ chī le shénme?**
What did you have for lunch?

→ 我们吃了自助餐。 **Wǒmen chī le zìzhùcān.**
We had a buffet.

做

zuò

亻 / 11 strokes

to do, to make,
to produce, to write,
to compose

*My mom **made**
my birthday cake.*

做功课	**zuò gōngkè**	do homework
做饭	**zuòfàn**	to prepare a meal
做事	**zuòshì**	to work
订做	**dìngzuò**	to custom-make
做客	**zuòkè**	to be a guest

Chinese Characters Writing Practice Pad—**Character #93**

我 订 做 了 一 把 椅 子。

也 替 我 订 做 一 把 吧。

→ 我订做了一把椅子。 **Wǒ dìngzuò le yì bǎ yǐzi.**
  I ordered a custom-made chair.

→ 也替我订做一把吧。 **Yě tì wǒ dìngzuò yì bǎ ba.**
  Order one for me as well.

少 ⺌ ⺌ 少 少 少 少

少

shǎo　few, less, to lack

小 / 4 strokes

*This drink has **less** sugar in it.*

少数	**shǎoshù**	few, minority
少量	**shǎoliàng**	a small amount
不少	**bùshǎo**	not few, many
减少	**jiǎnshǎo**	to lessen, to decrease

Chinese Characters Writing Practice Pad—**Character #94**

这	次	旅	行	要	带	多	少	钱	？
少	量	就	够	了	。				

→ 这次旅行要带多少钱？ **Zhè cì lǚxíng yào dài duōshao qián?** How much should I take on this trip?

→ 少量就够了。 **Shǎoliàng jiù gòu le.**
A small amount will do.

丿	口	曰	吖	吟	吃	吃	吃
吃							

吃

chī   to eat

口 / 6 strokes

Freddy eats a lot and often.

吃饭	**chīfàn**	to have a meal
吃完	**chīwán**	to finish eating
好吃	**hǎochī**	tasty, delicious
小吃	**xiǎochī**	snack, refreshments

Chinese Characters Writing Practice Pad—**Character #95**

街头的小吃很好吃。

是吗？我们也去吃。

→ 街头的小吃很好吃。 **Jiētóu de xiǎochī hěn hǎochī.**
The street snacks are yummy.

→ 是吗？我们也去吃。 **Shì ma? Wǒmen yě qù chī.**
Really? Let's go too.

后　厂　户　斤　后　后　后　后

后

后　　　後　(for "back, behind" meanings)
　　　　　Traditional

hòu　　back, behind; queen

口 / 6 strokes

*I put my books in the **back** of my bag.*

后来	**hòulái**	afterwards, later
后天	**hòutiān**	the day after tomorrow
后悔	**hòuhuǐ**	to regret; regret; regretful
落后	**luòhòu**	fallen behind, backward
皇后	**huánghòu**	queen

Chinese Characters Writing Practice Pad—**Character #96**

他 去 年 没 买 房 子 。

现 在 很 后 悔 吧 ！

→ 他去年没买房子。 **Tā qùnián méi mǎi fángzi.**
He didn't buy a flat last year.

→ 现在很后悔吧！ **Xiànzài hěn hòuhuǐ ba!**
Now he must be very regretful.

听

聽
Traditional

We **heard** the bell ringing, and prepared to go home.

tīng
口 / 7 strokes
to listen, to hear, to obey

听说	**tīngshuō**	one hears (that); hearsay
听众	**tīngzhòng**	audience, listeners
听懂	**tīngdǒng**	to understand
动听	**dòngtīng**	pleasant to listen to

Chinese Characters Writing Practice Pad—**Character #97**

她	没	有	接	电	话	。			
听	说	她	病	了	。				

→ 她没有接电话。 **Tā méiyǒu jiē diànhuà.**
She didn't answer the phone.

→ 听说她病了。 **Tīngshuō tā bìng le.** I heard that she is sick.

| 丿 | 人 | 仒 | 仐 | 会 | 会 | 会 | 会 |
| 会 | | | | | | | |

会 會
Traditional

huì to meet; meeting

人 / 6 strokes

*They have a **meeting** to discuss their travel plans.*

会员	**huìyuán**	member
会议	**huìyì**	meeting, conference
机会	**jīhuì**	opportunity
一会儿	**yīhuìr**	one moment

Chinese Characters Writing Practice Pad—**Character #98**

我	还	有	机	会	吗	？			
再	等	一	会	儿	吧	。			

→ 我还有机会吗？ **Wǒ háiyǒu jīhuì ma?**
Do I still have a chance?

→ 再等一会儿吧。 **Zài děng yíhuìr ba.**
Wait for a little while.

爫	爫	爫	爫	爫	爫	爫	爫
爱	爱	爱	爱	爱			

爱

愛
Traditional

ài
⺤ / 10 strokes

to love, to be
fond of; affection

*Some children
love dogs a lot.*

爱人	**àirén**	spouse, lover
爱好	**àihào**	to like; hobby
爱心	**àixīn**	kindness
可爱	**kě'ài**	cute, lovely
爱情	**àiqíng**	(romantic) love

Chinese Characters Writing Practice Pad—**Character #99**

他	是	个	很	有	爱	心	的	人	。
他	的	样	子	也	很	可	爱	。	

→ 他是个很有爱心的人。 **Tā shì gè hěn yǒu àixīn de rén.**
He is a kind-hearted person.

→ 他的样子也很可爱。 **Tā de yàngzi yě hěn kě'ài.**
His appearance is lovely too.

作　作　作　作　作　作　作　作

作　作

作

zuò

亻 / 7 strokes

to do, to write
or compose

*Emails are quick to **write**,
so we use them daily.*

作者	**zuòzhě**	author
作业	**zuòyè**	homework
工作	**gōngzuò**	work, task
合作	**hézuò**	to cooperate; cooperation

Chinese Characters Writing Practice Pad—**Character #100**

他做什么工作？

他写小说，是这本书的
作者。

→ 他做什么工作？ **Tā zuò shénme gōngzuò?**
What does he do (for a living)?

→ 他写小说，是这本书的作者。 **Tā xiě xiǎoshuō, shì zhè
běn shū de zuòzhě.** He writes novels. He is the author of
this book.

你

nǐ you

亻 / 7 strokes

*I love **you**.*

你的	**nǐ de**	your, yours
你们	**nǐmen**	you (plural)
你好	**nǐhǎo**	hello!, hi!, How are you?
迷你	**mínǐ**	mini (loanword)

Chinese Characters Writing Practice Pad—**Character #101**

你	的	迷	你	裙	好	漂	亮	。	
是	吗	？	不	太	短	吗	？		

→ 你的迷你裙好漂亮。 **Nǐ de mínǐ qún hǎo piàoliang!**
Your mini-skirt is very pretty.

→ 是吗？不太短吗？ **Shì ma? Bú tài duǎn ma?**
Is it? Not too short?

ノ	二	千	禾	禾	禾	和	和
和	和	和					

和

hé   harmonious; and

口 / 8 strokes

*I have a smartphone
and a computer.*

和平	**hépíng**	peace, peaceful
和尚	**héshang**	Buddhist monk
温和	**wēnhé**	mild, gentle, moderate
总和	**zǒnghé**	sum, total

Chinese Characters Writing Practice Pad—**Character #102**

小	和	尚	性	格	温	和	。		
他	和	人	可	以	和	平	共	处	。

→ 小和尚性格温和。 **Xiǎo héshang xìnggé wēnhé.**
The little monk has a mild temperament.

→ 他和人可以和平共处。 **Tā hé rén kěyǐ hépínggòngchǔ.**
He gets along harmoniously with people.

一	十	才	木	朩	村	柯	椅
椅	椅	椅	椅	椅	椅	椅	

椅

yǐ   chair

木 / 12 strokes

A wheelchair is a special chair.

椅子	**yǐzi**	chair
轮椅	**lúnyǐ**	wheelchair
木椅	**mùyǐ**	wooden chair
椅套	**yǐtào**	chair cover

Chinese Characters Writing Practice Pad—**Character #103**

我 把 椅 套 弄 脏 了 ！

拿 去 干 洗 吧。

→ 我把椅套弄脏了！ **Wǒ bǎ yǐtào nòng zāng le!**
  I dirtied the chair cover.
→ 拿去干洗吧。 **Ná qù gānxǐ ba.** Take it for dry cleaning.

一	左	车	车	车	车	车

车　車
Traditional

chē　car, vehicle

车 / 4 strokes

It is fun to go driving in this car.

火车	**huǒchē**	train
车站	**chēzhàn**	bus/train station
车费	**chēfèi**	passenger fare
堵车	**dǔchē**	traffic jam
出租车	**chūzūchē**	taxi

Chinese Characters Writing Practice Pad—**Character #104**

十分钟就到火车站吗？

不堵车就可以。

→ 十分钟就到火车站吗？ **Shí fēnzhōng jiù dào huǒchēzhàn ma?** Can we get to the train station in 10 minutes?

→ 不堵车就可以。 **Bù dǔchē jiù kěyǐ.**
We can if there is no traffic jam.

刁	刁	刁	刖	刄	那	那	那
那							

那

nà

阝 / 6 strokes

that, those; then
(in that case)

Those flags decorate the sports field.

那么	**nàme**	so
那个	**nàge**	that one
那些	**nàxiē**	those
那时候	**nà shíhou**	at that time

Chinese Characters Writing Practice Pad—**Character #105**

那些地方你都去过吗？

都去过。那时候我还小！

→ 那些地方你都去过吗？ **Nàxiē dìfāng nǐ dōu qù guò ma?**
Have you been to all those places?

→ 都去过。那时候我还小！ **Dōu qù guò. Nà shíhou wǒ hái xiǎo!** Yes, when I was small.

| 亅 | 仁 | 钅 | 钅 | 金 | 钅 | 钔 | 钔 |
| 钟 | 钟 | 钟 | 钟 | | | | |

钟　鐘
Traditional

zhōng　clock, o'clock, bell

钅 / 9 strokes

We heard the **bell** ringing.

分钟	**fēnzhōng**	minute (time)
闹钟	**nàozhōng**	alarm clock
警钟	**jǐngzhōng**	alarm bell
钟表	**zhōngbiǎo**	clock

Chinese Characters Writing Practice Pad—**Character #106**

你	为	什	么	迟	到	？			
我	的	闹	钟	坏	了	。			

→ 你为什么迟到？ **Nǐ wèishénme chídào?** Why are you late?

→ 我的闹钟坏了。 **Wǒ de nàozhōng huài le!**
My alarm clock didn't work.

认

认

认

认 **Traditional**

*The child **recognizes** his mom.*

rèn
讠 / 4 strokes

to recognize,
to know, to admit

认为	**rènwéi**	to believe, to think
认真	**rènzhēn**	conscientious, earnest
认识	**rènshi**	to know; knowledge
否认	**fǒurèn**	to deny; denial

Chinese Characters Writing Practice Pad—**Character #107**

我	认	识	这	个	歌	手	！		
他	认	识	你	吗	？				

→ 我认识这个歌手！ **Wǒ rènshi zhège gēshǒu!**
I know this singer!

→ 他认识你吗？ **Tā rènshi nǐ ma?** Does he know you?

丶	讠	讠＇	识	识	识	识	识
识	识						

识 識
Traditional

shí   to know; knowledge

讠 / 7 strokes

*Do you **know** how to play Sudoku?*

识别	**shíbié**	to distinguish, to discern
知识	**zhīshi**	knowledge
常识	**chángshí**	common sense, general knowledge
共识	**gòngshí**	common understanding, consensus

Chinese Characters Writing Practice Pad—**Character #108**

你	开	除	他	了	吗	?			
他	一	点	儿	常	识	都	没	有	。

→ 你开除他了吗？ **Nǐ kāichú tā le ma?** You fired him?

→ 他一点儿常识都没有。 **Tā yìdiǎnr chángshí dōu méiyǒu.**
He absolutely has no common sense.

﹀	记	记	语	语	语	语	语
语	语	语	语				

语　語
Traditional

木制品区

yǔ　language, speech

讠 / 9 strokes

*What **language** is on the sign?*

母语	**mǔyǔ**	mother tongue
外语	**wàiyǔ**	foreign language
双语	**shuāngyǔ**	bilingual
语气	**yǔqì**	tone, manner of speaking

Chinese Characters Writing Practice Pad—**Character #109**

你的母语是什么？

英语是我的母语。

→ 你的母语是什么？ **Nǐ de mǔyǔ shì shénme?**
What is your mother tongue?

→ 英语是我的母语。 **Yīngyǔ shì wǒ de mǔyǔ.**
English is my mother tongue.

| 丿 | 冂 | 冃 | 日 | 日一 | 时 | 时 | 时 |

| 时 | 时 | | | | | | |

时

時
Traditional

shí

日 / 7 strokes

time, hour, season, period

*The **time** is 7:00 now.*

时间	**shíjiān**	time, period
时候	**shíhou**	length of time, period
时机	**shíjī**	opportunity
时髦	**shímáo**	modern, fashionable

Chinese Characters Writing Practice Pad—**Character #110**

我	们	什	么	时	候	买	房	子	？
你	说	呢	？						

→ 我们什么时候买房子？ **Wǒmen shénme shíhou mǎi fángzi?**
When are we buying a house?

→ 你说呢？ **Nǐ shuō ne?** What is your view?

读 读 读 读 读 读 读

读 读 读 读 读

读

讀
Traditional

dú   to read, to study

讠 / 10 strokes

*I **read** this book many times.*

读者	**dúzhě**	reader
读书	**dúshū**	to read a book, to study
读音	**dúyīn**	pronunciation
阅读	**yuèdú**	to read; reading

Chinese Characters Writing Practice Pad—**Character #111**

你还在读书吗？

没有，已经工作了。

→ 你还在读书吗？ **Nǐ hái zài dúshū ma?**
Are you still studying?

→ 没有，已经工作了。 **Méiyǒu, yǐjīng gōngzuò le.**
No, I am working now.

丿	二	牛	生	步	先	先	先
先							

先

xiān

儿 / 6 strokes

early, prior, former, in advance, first

*I was **first** to finish the exam.*

先生	**xiānsheng**	mister, teacher, husband
先进	**xiānjìn**	advanced
首先	**shǒuxiān**	first, in the first place
优先	**yōuxiān**	to have priority

Chinese Characters Writing Practice Pad—**Character #112**

这	所	学	校	非	常	先	进	。	
我	想	在	这	儿	上	学	。		

→ 这所学校非常先进。 **Zhè suǒ xuéxiào fēicháng xiānjìn.**
This school is very advanced.

→ 我想在这儿上学。 **Wǒ xiǎng zài zhèr shàngxué.**
I would like to study here.

丿	仨	仨	仨	全	钅	钅	钱
钱	钱	钱	钱	钱			

钱

錢
Traditional

qián　　coin, money

钅 / 10 strokes

*We need **money** for daily living.*

钱包	**qiánbāo**	purse, wallet
有钱	**yǒuqián**	wealthy
零钱	**língqián**	small change, pocket money
付钱	**fùqián**	to pay money

Chinese Characters Writing Practice Pad—**Character #113**

我	的	钱	包	不	见	了	！		
你	是	开	玩	笑	吗	？			

→ 我的钱包不见了！ **Wǒ de qiánbāo bújiàn le!**
My wallet has disappeared!

→ 你是开玩笑吗？ **Nǐ shì kāi wánxiào ma?** Are you kidding?

八

bā eight, 8

八 / 2 strokes

This pool looks like the number 8.

八月	**Bāyuè**	August
八十	**bāshí**	eighty, 80
十八	**shíbā**	eighteen, 18
第八	**dì-bā**	eighth (sequence)

Chinese Characters Writing Practice Pad—**Character #114**

他 下 个 星 期 十 八 岁 了 。

小 朋 友 长 得 真 快 ！

→ 他下个星期十八岁了。 **Tā xià gè xīngqī shíbā suì le.**
He'll turn 18 next week.

→ 小朋友长得真快！ **Xiǎopéngyou zhǎng de zhēn kuài!**
Children grow up fast!

六

liù   six, 6

八 / 4 strokes

*We baked **six** pies.*

六月	**Liùyuè**	June
六十	**liùshí**	sixty, 60
十六	**shíliù**	sixteen, 16
第六	**dì-liù**	sixth

Chinese Characters Writing Practice Pad—**Character #115**

我	今	年	六	月	会	去	新	加	坡
。									
我	去	年	去	过	了	。			

→ 我今年六月会去新加坡。 **Wǒ jīnnián Liùyuè huì qù Xīnjiāpō.** I'm going to Singapore this June.

→ 我去年去过了。 **Wǒ qùnián qù guò le.** I went last year.

一	十	土	耂	考	老	老	老
老							

老

lǎo   old, aged

耂 / 6 strokes

*This **old** man is very healthy.*

老师	**lǎoshī**	teacher
老婆	**lǎopo**	wife (colloq.)
老公	**lǎogong**	husband (colloq.)
古老	**gǔlǎo**	ancient

Chinese Characters Writing Practice Pad—**Character #116**

北	京	是	一	个	古	老	的	城	市
。									
我	很	想	去	看	看	。			

→ 北京是一个古老的城市。 **Běijīng shì yí gè gǔlǎo de chéngshì.** Beijing is an ancient city.

→ 我很想去看看。 **Wǒ hěn xiǎng qù kànkan.** I would like to go there.

`	二	亍	文	文	议	这	这
这	这						

这 這
Traditional

zhè this

辶 / 7 strokes

This can be used to measure time.

这个	**zhège**	this, this one
这位	**zhèwèi**	this person
这边	**zhèbiān**	this side, here
这里	**zhèlǐ**	here

Chinese Characters Writing Practice Pad—**Character #117**

我 的 钥 匙 不 见 了 ！

你 的 钥 匙 就 在 这 里 了 ！

→ 我的钥匙不见了！ **Wǒ de yàoshi bújiàn le!**
My key has disappeared.

→ 你的钥匙就在这里了！ **Nǐ de yàoshi jiù zài zhèlǐ le!**
Your key is right here.

一	丆	刀	冇	再	再	再	再
再							

再

zài

冂 / 6 strokes

again, once more;
re-, another

再见!

*"See you again!"
in Chinese*

再见	**zàijiàn**	see you again
一再	**yízài**	repeatedly
再来	**zàilái**	to come again
不再	**búzài**	no more, no longer
再次	**zàicì**	one more time

Chinese Characters Writing Practice Pad—**Character #118**

有	时	间	再	喝	杯	茶	吗	？	
今	天	不	行	，		下	次	吧	。

→ 有时间再喝杯茶吗？ **Yǒu shíjiān zài hē bēi chá ma?**
Do you have time for tea?

→ 今天不行，下次吧。 **Jīntiān bù xíng, xiàcì ba.**
Not today, next time.

丶	⼧	写	写	写	写	写	写

写 寫
Traditional

A BIG FAT MOUSE

He **writes** in capital letters.

xiě   to write

⼧ / 5 strokes

写信	**xiěxìn**	to write a letter
写字	**xiězì**	writing
描写	**miáoxiě**	to describe; description
写法	**xiěfǎ**	style of writing

Chinese Characters Writing Practice Pad—**Character #119**

我	不	写	信	,	只	写	电	邮	。
我	不	会	用	电	脑	。			

→ 我不写信，只写电邮。 **Wǒ bù xiěxìn, zhǐ xiě diànyóu.**
I don't write letters, only emails.

→ 我不会用电脑。 **Wǒ bú huì yòng diànnǎo.**
I don't know how to use a computer.

一 寸 扌 打 打 打 打 打

打

dǎ　　to hit, to break

扌 / 5 strokes

*The cat **broke** my lovely plates.*

打电话	**dǎ diànhuà**	to make a telephone call
打篮球	**dǎ lánqiú**	to play basketball
打扫	**dǎsǎo**	to clean up; clean-up
打算	**dǎsuàn**	to plan, to intend; plan

Chinese Characters Writing Practice Pad—**Character #120**

他 明 天 上 学 吗 ？

你 打 电 话 问 一 问 ！

→ 他明天上学吗？ **Tā míngtiān shàngxué ma?**
Is he going to school tomorrow?

→ 你打电话问一问！ **Nǐ dǎ diànhuà wènyiwèn!**
You'd better call him and ask!

| ﹀ | 二 | 亠 | 立 | 产 | 产 | 产 | 商 |
| 商 | 商 | 商 | 商 | 商 | 商 | | |

商

shāng   commerce, trade

口 / 11 strokes

*Long ago people used seashells as money to do **trade**.*

商店	**shāngdiàn**	shop
商业	**shāngyè**	commerce, business, trade
商人	**shāngrén**	businessperson
商学院	**shāngxuéyuàn**	business school
商量	**shāngliang**	to discuss

Chinese Characters Writing Practice Pad—**Character #121**

我	想	给	她	买	件	外	套	。	
附	近	有	家	商	店	。			

→ 我想给她买件外套。 **Wǒ xiǎng gěi tā mǎi jiàn wàitào.** I'd like to buy her a jacket.

→ 附近有家商店。 **Fùjìn yǒu jiā shāngdiàn.** There is a store nearby.

ﾉ	刀	冂	日	明	明	明	明
明	明	明					

明

míng   bright, clear

日 / 8 strokes

*The night is **bright** with shiny stars.*

明显	**míngxiǎn**	clear, obvious
明白	**míngbai**	to understand, to realize
明亮	**míngliàng**	bright, shining
聪明	**cōngming**	clever, bright

Chinese Characters Writing Practice Pad—**Character #122**

老	师	最	喜	欢	他	。			
他	是	班	上	最	聪	明	的	。	

→ 老师最喜欢他。 **Lǎoshī zuì xǐhuan tā.**
The teachers like him most.

→ 他是班上最聪明的。 **Tā shì bānshang zuì cōngmíng de.**
He is the cleverest in class.

飞	飞	飞	飞	飞	飞		

飞 飛
Traditional

fēi   to fly

飞 / 3 strokes

*We **fly** to Bangkok by Thai Airways.*

飞机	**fēijī**	airplane
飞行	**fēixíng**	to fly; flying
起飞	**qǐfēi**	to take off (aircraft); take-off
直飞	**zhífēi**	direct flight

Chinese Characters Writing Practice Pad—**Character #123**

飞 行 时 间 多 长 ？

三 个 小 时 。

→ 飞行时间多长？ **Fēixíng shíjiān duō cháng?**
How long is the flight?

→ 三个小时。 **Sān gè xiǎoshí.** Three hours.

ノ	口	日	日	旦	早	是	是
是	是	是	是				

是

shì to be; yes

日 / 9 strokes

Yes, she is Irish.

凡是	**fánshì**	each and every, every, all
但是	**dànshì**	but, however
总是	**zǒngshì**	always
还是	**háishì**	still

Chinese Characters Writing Practice Pad—**Character #124**

为	什	么	你	总	是	迟	到	?	
我	病	了	！						

→ 为什么你总是迟到？ **Wèishénme nǐ zǒngshì chídào?**
Why are you always late?

→ 我病了！ **Wǒ bìng le!** I am not well.

ᵧ	ㅁ	吕	吢	吣	吶	吜	吜
喝	喝	喝	喝	喝	喝	喝	

喝

1. **hē** to drink
2. **hè** to shout loudly

口 / 12 strokes

*We love **to drink** cold lemonade when the day is hot.*

喝咖啡	**hē kāfēi**	to drink coffee
喝茶	**hē chá**	to drink tea
好喝	**hǎohē**	tasty (drinks)
难喝	**nánhē**	unpleasant to drink
大喝	**dà hè**	to shout loudly

Chinese Characters Writing Practice Pad—**Character #125**

我 每 天 都 喝 咖 啡 。

那 对 身 体 好 吗 ？

→ 我每天都喝咖啡。 **Wǒ měitiān dōu hē kāfēi.**
  I drink coffee every day.

→ 那对身体好吗？ **Nà duì shēntǐ hǎo ma?**
  Is it good for the body?

一　ナ　大　大　大　大

大

dà

大 / 3 strokes

big, large, great, older (than); greatly

*Did you know that the blue whale is very **big**?*

大家	**dàjiā**	everyone
大型	**dàxíng**	large-scale
大方	**dàfāng**	generous
加大	**jiādà**	extra large

Chinese Characters Writing Practice Pad—**Character #126**

有加大码吗？

没有，只有中码。

→ 有加大码吗？ **Yǒu jiādà mǎ ma?** Any extra-large size?

→ 没有，只有中码。 **Méiyǒu, zhǐyǒu zhōngmǎ.**
No, only medium size.

㇆	二	干	天	天	天	天

天

tiān　　day, sky, heaven

大 / 4 strokes

*The **sky** looks cloudy.*

天气	**tiānqì**	weather
蓝天	**lántiān**	blue sky
明天	**míngtiān**	tomorrow
昨天	**zuótiān**	yesterday
天空	**tiānkōng**	sky

Chinese Characters Writing Practice Pad—**Character #127**

明	天	会	下	雨	吗	？			
我	要	看	看	天	气	预	报	。	

→ 明天会下雨吗？ **Míngtiān huì xiàyǔ ma?**
Is it going to rain tomorrow?

→ 我要看看天气预报。 **Wǒ yào kànkan tiānqì yùbào.**
I have to look at the weather forecast.

冷

lěng cold

冫 / 7 strokes

It must be **cold** up
on the mountains.

冷静	**lěngjìng**	calm, cool-headed
冷气	**lěngqì**	air conditioning
冰冷	**bīnglěng**	ice-cold
寒冷	**hánlěng**	cold (climate), very cold

Chinese Characters Writing Practice Pad—**Character #128**

天气真冷！

是啊，我穿了两件外套
！

→ 天气真冷！ **Tiānqì zhēn lěng!** It is really cold!

→ 是啊，我穿了两件外套！ **Shì a, wǒ chuān le liǎng jiàn wàitào!** Yes, I put on two coats.

一	ナ	大	太	太	太	太

太

tài

大 / 4 strokes

highest, greatest; too (much)

*There are **too** many clothes for the suitcase.*

太忙　　　**tàimáng**　　too busy
太阳　　　**tàiyáng**　　sun
太空　　　**tàikōng**　　outer space
太过份　　**tài guòfèn**　over the top

Chinese Characters Writing Practice Pad—**Character #129**

每	天	工	作	十	二	个	小	时	？
是	啊	，		太	过	份	了	。	

→ 每天工作十二个小时？ **Měitiān gōngzuò shíèr gè xiǎoshí?**
Working 12 hours a day?

→ 是啊，太过份了。 **Shì a, tài guòfèn le.** Yes, it's over the top.

几　丿　几　几　几　几

几

幾[1]
Traditional

1. **jǐ**　　several, how many/much; almost

2. **jī**　　small table

几 / 2 strokes

How much for five pens?

几个	**jǐge**	a few, several; how many
几次	**jǐcì**	several times
几乎	**jīhū**	almost
茶几	**chájī**	small side-table, coffee table

Chinese Characters Writing Practice Pad—**Character #130**

为	什	么	赶	他	出	去	？		
他	几	乎	把	茶	几	推	翻	了	。

→ 为什么赶他出去？ **Wèishénme gǎn tā chūqù?**
Why kicked him out?

→ 他几乎把茶几推翻了。 **Tā jīhū bǎ chájī tuī fān le.**
He almost knocked over the coffee table.

女　女　女　女　女　女

女

nǚ　female, woman,
女 / 3 strokes　daughter

*The woman has a
female child.*

女孩　**nǚhái**　girl
女生　**nǚshēng**　female student
女朋友　**nǚ péngyou**　girlfriend
美女　**měinǚ**　beautiful woman

Chinese Characters Writing Practice Pad—**Character #131**

我姐姐生了一个孩子。

是男孩还是女孩？

→ 我姐姐生了一个孩子。 **Wǒ jiějie shēng le yí gè háizi.**
My elder sister has given birth to a child.

→ 是男孩还是女孩？ **Shì nánhái háishi nǚhái?**
Is it a boy or a girl?

〈	〈	〈	〈	〈	〈	好	好

好

好

1. **hǎo**   good, well, proper
2. **hào**   to be good at; interest

女 / 6 strokes

*The video games are **good** and fun.*

好像	**hǎoxiàng**	as if, to seem like
好朋友	**hǎo péngyou**	close friend
美好	**měihǎo**	beautiful
爱好	**àihào**	hobby, interest

这酒店真舒服！

好像到了自己家一样。

→ 这酒店真舒服！ **Zhè jiǔdiàn zhēn shūfu!**
This hotel is really comfortable.

→ 好像到了自己家一样。 **Hǎoxiàng dào le zìjǐ jiā yíyàng.**
It's like being in our own home.

| 丿 | 刀 | 月 | 月 | 目 | 目 | 目 | 眄 |

| 眄 | 眄 | 眄 | 睡 | 睡 | 睡 | 睡 | 睡 |

睡

shuì   to sleep, to lie down

目 / 13 strokes

*He **sleeps** with a light on.*

睡觉	**shuìjiào**	to sleep; sleep
睡懒觉	**shuì lǎnjiào**	to sleep in
睡衣	**shuìyī**	pajamas
小睡	**xiǎoshuì**	to nap; nap

Chinese Characters Writing Practice Pad—**Character #133**

可	以	看	电	影	吗	?			
很	晚	了	,		快	去	睡	觉	。

→ 可以看电影吗？ **Kěyǐ kàn diànyǐng ma?**
Can I watch a movie?

→ 很晚了，快去睡觉。 **Hěn wǎn le, kuài qù shuìjiào.**
It's late, go to sleep now.

𠂊	厶	台	自	自	自	自	能
能	能	能	能	能			

能

néng

月 / 10 strokes

can, to be able to; possibly; ability

*This person **can** do the high jump.*

能力	**nénglì**	capability, ability
可能	**kěnéng**	possible
技能	**jìnéng**	technical ability
功能	**gōngnéng**	function, capability

Chinese Characters Writing Practice Pad—**Character #134**

你	不	去	美	国	留	学	吗	？	
钱	不	够	，		不	可	能	了	。

→ 你不去美国留学吗？ **Nǐ bú qù Měiguó liúxué ma?**
Are you not going to the States for further studies?

→ 钱不够，不可能了。 **Qián bú gòu, bù kěnéng le.**
I don't have enough money, not possible now.

→	丁	工	工	工	工		

工

gōng　work

工 / 3 strokes

*This **work** needs careful attention.*

工作	**gōngzuò**	work
工厂	**gōngchǎng**	factory
工具	**gōngjù**	tool, instrument
工人	**gōngrén**	worker
义工	**yìgōng**	volunteer, voluntary work

Chinese Characters Writing Practice Pad—**Character #135**

她是个善良的人。

她有时间就做义工。

→ 她是个善良的人。 **Tā shì gè shànliáng de rén.**
She is a kind-hearted lady.

→ 她有时间就做义工。 **Tā yǒu shíjiān jiù zuò yìgōng.**
She does voluntary work whenever she has time.

⌐	三	丢	王	玌	玏	玏	现
现	现	现					

现　現
Traditional

xiàn　to appear; now

见 / 8 strokes

Sometimes double rainbows **appear** *in the sky.*

现金	**xiànjīn**	cash
发现	**fāxiàn**	to find, to discover
出现	**chūxiàn**	to appear; appearance
表现	**biǎoxiàn**	to show, to show off; performance

Chinese Characters Writing Practice Pad—**Character #136**

信用卡可以吗？

不行，我们只收现金。

→ 信用卡可以吗？ **Xìnyòngkǎ kěyǐ ma?** Is credit card ok?

→ 不行，我们只收现金。 **Bùxíng, wǒmen zhǐ shōu xiànjīn.**
No, we only take cash.

丶	亠	亠	衣	衣	衣	衣	衣
衣							

衣

yī　　clothes

衣 / 6 strokes

*He has a lot of **clothes** on.*

衣服	**yīfu**	clothes
衣柜	**yīguì**	wardrobe
内衣	**nèiyī**	undergarment, underwear
毛衣	**máoyī**	woolen garment

Chinese Characters Writing Practice Pad—**Character #137**

我	们	今	年	暑	假	去	澳	洲	。
那	你	需	要	多	带	一	点	衣	服
。									

→ 我们今年暑假去澳洲。 **Wǒmen jīnnián shǔjià qù Àozhōu.**
This summer holiday we are going to Australia.

→ 那你需要多带一点衣服。 **Nà nǐ xūyào duō dài yìdiǎn yīfu.**
Then you need to bring more clothes.

⼍	口	日	日	旦	里	里	里
里	里						

里 　裡 (only for meaning of "inside")

Traditional

lǐ

里 / 7 strokes

measure of length, approx. 500 m; neighborhood, inside

The campsite is 10 *li* from the church.

里面	**lǐmiàn**	inside
那里	**nàlǐ**	there
公里	**gōnglǐ**	kilometer
英里	**yīnglǐ**	mile

Chinese Characters Writing Practice Pad—**Character #138**

到火车站有多远？

半公里吧。

→ 到火车站有多远？ **Dào huǒchēzhàn yǒu duō yuǎn?**
How far is the train station?

→ 半公里吧。 **Bàn gōnglǐ ba.** Half a kilometer.

| ノ | 八 | 分 | 分 | 分 | 分 | 分 | |

分

fēn

刀 / 4 strokes

to divide, to allocate; minute, credits

*Please **divide** the sweets equally among your five friends.*

分类	**fēnlèi**	to classify; classification
分开	**fēnkāi**	to separate
满分	**mǎnfēn**	full marks
学分	**xuéfēn**	course credits

Chinese Characters Writing Practice Pad—**Character #139**

我	先	付	还	是	分	开	账	单	？
分	开	吧	，	方	便	计	算	。	

→ 我先付还是分开账单？ **Wǒ xiān fù háishi fēnkāi zhàng-dān?** Shall I pay first, or separate bills?

→ 分开吧，方便计算。 **Fēnkāi ba, fāngbiàn jìsuàn.** Separately, it's easier to calculate.

ㄑ	ㄠ	女	如	如	姐	姐	姐
姐	姐	姐					

姐

jiě   older sister

女 / 8 strokes

*My **older sister** has big eyes.*

姐姐	**jiějie**	older sister
姐妹	**jiěmèi**	sisters
姐夫	**jiěfu**	older sister's husband
大姐	**dàjiě**	oldest sister; address for someone older than oneself

Chinese Characters Writing Practice Pad—**Character #140**

大姐，你的表演很精采。

你太客气了。

→ 大姐，你的表演很精采。 **Dàjiě, nǐ de biǎoyǎn hěn jīngcǎi.**
Older sister, your performance is superb.

→ 你太客气了。 **Nǐ tài kèqi le.** You are too polite.

㇏	丿	刂	师	师	师	师	师
师							

师

師
Traditional

shī　teacher, master, expert

巾 / 6 strokes

*Mr Chen is a **master** of cooking.*

师傅	**shīfu**	master
厨师	**chúshī**	chef
律师	**lùshī**	lawyer
导师	**dǎoshī**	tutor, academic advisor

Chinese Characters Writing Practice Pad—**Character #141**

我 想 当 厨 师 。

你 先 要 找 一 个 好 师 傅 。

→ 我想当厨师。 **Wǒ xiǎng dāng chúshī.** I want to be a chef.

→ 你先要找一个好师傅。 **Nǐ xiān yào zhǎo yí gè hǎo shīfu.**
You have to first find a good master.

月 刀 月 月 月 月 月

月

shī   moon, month

月 / 4 strokes

*Christmas is celebrated in the **month** of December.*

月亮	**yuèliang**	moon
月薪	**yuèxīn**	monthly salary
蜜月	**mìyuè**	honeymoon
满月	**mǎnyuè**	reaching one month (baby's)

Chinese Characters Writing Practice Pad—**Character #142**

婴儿多大了？

刚满月。

→ 婴儿多大了？ **Yīng'ér duō dà le?** How old is the baby?
→ 刚满月。 **Gāng mǎnyuè.** Just one month.

一	大	才	有	有	有	有	有
有							

有

yǒu   to have, to exist, to be

月 / 6 strokes

*I **have** four goldfish at home.*

有效   **yǒuxiào**   effective
有机   **yǒujī**   organic
没有   **méiyǒu**   don't have, there isn't
只有   **zhǐyǒu**   only

Chinese Characters Writing Practice Pad—**Character #143**

有	机	食	品	真	的	有	效	吗	？
不	知	道	。						

→ 有机食品真的有效吗？ **Yǒujī shípǐn zhēn de yǒuxiào ma?** Are organic foods really effective?

→ 不知道。 **Bù zhīdào.** I don't know.

年

nián   year

丿 / 6 strokes

年纪	**niánjì**	age
年轻	**niánqīng**	young
年级	**niánjí**	year, grade (school)
新年	**xīnnián**	New Year
去年	**qùnián**	last year

Welcome 2017

*Fireworks were lit at the start of a new **year**.*

Chinese Characters Writing Practice Pad—**Character #144**

我	年	纪	不	小	啦	！			
你	看	起	来	还	很	年	轻	。	

→ 我年纪不小啦！ **Wǒ niánjì bù xiǎo la!** I am not young!

→ 你看起来还很年轻。 **Nǐ kànqǐlái hái hěn niánqīng.**
You still look very young.

| 一 | 十 | 才 | 木 | 本 | 本 | 本 | 本 |

本

běn

木 / 5 strokes

origin, source; classifier for books, files, etc.

*Three **volumes** of the encyclopedia*

本地	**běndì**	local
基本	**jīběn**	fundamental, elementary
笔记本	**bǐjìběn**	notebook
样本	**yàngběn**	sample, specimen

Chinese Characters Writing Practice Pad—**Character #145**

你在找什么？

我的笔记本。

→ 你在找什么？ **Nǐ zài zhǎo shénme?**
What are you looking for?
→ 我的笔记本。 **Wǒ de bǐjìběn.** My notebook.

丶	亠	广	庁	庀	庀	店	店
店	店	店					

店

diàn   shop, store

广 / 8 strokes

*These **shops** are popular.*

饭店	**fàndiàn**	restaurant, hotel
书店	**shūdiàn**	bookstore
花店	**huādiàn**	flower shop
网店	**wǎngdiàn**	online shop

Chinese Characters Writing Practice Pad—**Character #146**

哪儿有花店？

对面书店旁边就是。

→ 哪儿有花店？ **Nǎr yǒu huādiàn?** Where is the florist?

→ 对面书店旁边就是。 **Duìmiàn shūdiàn pángbiān jiù shì.**
The florist is adjacent to the bookstore opposite us.

一	十	才	木	朷	机	机	机
机							

机

機
Traditional

jī   machine

木 / 6 strokes

*This is a photocopying **machine**.*

机票	**jīpiào**	air ticket
机场	**jīchǎng**	airport
司机	**sījī**	driver, chauffeur
数码	**shùmǎ**	digital camera
照相机	**zhàoxiàngjī**	

Chinese Characters Writing Practice Pad—**Character #147**

到	机	场	了	！					
我	好	像	没	带	机	票	。		

→ 到机场了！ **Dào jīchǎng le!** We arrived at the airport.

→ 我好像没带机票。 **Wǒ hǎoxiàng méi dài jīpiào.**
I don't seem to have my plane ticket.

白

bái   white, blank

白 / 5 strokes

E_EPH__T

*Fill in the **blanks** with the missing letters.*

白天	**báitiān**	daytime
白菜	**báicài**	cabbage
苍白	**cāngbái**	pale
空白	**kòngbái**	blank

Chinese Characters Writing Practice Pad—**Character #148**

你	白	天	还	是	晚	上	工	作	？
我	通	常	都	是	白	天	工	作	。

→ 你白天还是晚上工作？ **Nǐ báitiān háishi wǎnshang gōngzuò?** Do you work in the daytime or at night?

→ 我通常都是白天工作。 **Wǒ tōngcháng dōu shì báitiān gōngzuò.** I usually work in the day.

一	二	王	王	玉	玎	玗	班
班	班	班	班	班			

班

bān   class, work shift

王 / 10 strokes

*Mike works the night **shift**.*

班级	**bānjí**	class level at school, grade
班长	**bānzhǎng**	class monitor
航班	**hángbān**	scheduled flight, flight number
加班	**jiābān**	to work overtime

Chinese Characters Writing Practice Pad—**Character #149**

您 的 航 班 什 么 时 候 到 ？

明 天 下 午 五 点 半 。

→ 您的航班什么时候到？ **Nín de hángbān shénme shíhou dào?** When will your flight arrive?

→ 明天下午五点半。 **Míngtiān xiàwǔ wǔ diǎn bàn.** 5:30 tomorrow afternoon.

乛	彐	彐	丯	丯3	邦	帮	帮
帮	帮	帮	帮				

帮　幫
Traditional

*They **help** to move the chairs.*

bāng

巾 / 9 strokes

to help, to support;
group, gang

帮助	**bāngzhù**	to help; help
帮忙	**bāngmáng**	to help; assistance
帮手	**bāngshou**	to lend a hand; assistant, helper
一帮人	**yì bāng rén**	a gang of person

Chinese Characters Writing Practice Pad—**Character #150**

谢 谢 你 的 帮 忙 。

不 客 气 。

→ 谢谢你的帮忙。 **Xièxie nǐ de bāngmáng.**
Thanks for your help.

→ 不客气。 **Bú kèqi.** It's my pleasure.

一	寸	才	扌	扫	报	报	报
报	报						

报　報
Traditional

bào
扌 / 7 strokes

to announce, to inform;
report, newspaper

*We read the
newspaper
every morning.*

报告	**bàogào**	to report; report
报纸	**bàozhǐ**	newspaper
日报	**rìbào**	daily newspaper
报酬	**bàochou**	reward, renumeration
报到	**bàodào**	to report for duty

Chinese Characters Writing Practice Pad—**Character #151**

你今天看报纸了吗？

还没看呢。

→ 你今天看报纸了吗？ **Nǐ jīntiān kàn bàozhǐ le ma?**
Have you read today's newspaper?

→ 还没看呢。 **Hái méi kàn ne.** Not yet.

| ㇗ | ㇄ | ㇄㇒ | 比 | 比 | 比 | 比 | |

比

bǐ

比 / 4 strokes

to compare,
to contrast

*The housewife **compares**
the price of oranges
before she buys them.*

比较	**bǐjiào**	to compare; relatively
比赛	**bǐsài**	competition, match
比如	**bǐrú**	for instance, such as
对比	**duìbǐ**	to contrast; contrast
比例	**bǐlì**	proportion, scale

Chinese Characters Writing Practice Pad—**Character #152**

你	看	足	球	比	赛	了	吗	？	
没	看	，		没	时	间	看	。	

→ 你看足球比赛了吗？ **Nǐ kàn zúqiú bǐsài le ma?**
Did you watch the football match?

→ 没看，没时间看。 **Méi kàn, méi shíjiān kàn.**
No, I had no time.

| 丿 | 亻 | 仁 | 仁 | 佢 | 佢 | 佢 | 便 |
| 便 | 便 | 便 | 便 | | | | |

便

1. **biàn**   suitable, convenient
2. **pián**   cheap

亻 / 9 strokes

*This is a **convenient** place to park the car.*

便宜	**piányi**	cheap
方便	**fāngbiàn**	convenient
顺便	**shùnbiàn**	conveniently, without extra effort
随便	**suíbiàn**	whatever one prefers, casual

Chinese Characters Writing Practice Pad—**Character #153**

你想吃点什么？

随便什么都可以。

→ 你想吃点什么？ **Nǐ xiǎng chī diǎn shénme?**
What would you like to eat?

→ 随便什么都可以。 **Suíbiàn shénme dōu kěyǐ.**
Anything will do.

一	三	丰	圭	声	表	表	表
表	表	表					

表　錶
Traditional

biǎo　surface, form, watch

衣 / 8 strokes

*The man has a
stylish wrist **watch**.*

手表	**shǒubiǎo**	wrist watch
钟表	**zhōngbiǎo**	clock
表格	**biǎogé**	form, chart
表演	**biǎoyǎn**	to perform; performance

Chinese Characters Writing Practice Pad—**Character #154**

请 填 一 张 表 格。

好 的， 请 给 我 一 张 。

→ 请填一张表格。 **Qǐng tián yì zhāng biǎogé.**
Please fill in a form first.

→ 好的，请给我一张。 **Hǎo de, qǐng gěi wǒ yì zhāng.**
Ok, please give me a form.

丿	口	口	另	另	别	别	别
别	别						

别

bié

刂 / 7 strokes

to leave, to distinguish; don't ...!

*The child does not want her mom to **leave** her.*

特别	**tèbié**	particularly; special
性别	**xìngbié**	gender
区别	**qūbié**	to distinguish; difference
别的	**biéde**	else, other

这 两 顶 帽 子 没 区 别。

别 动， 让 我 看 看。

→ 这两顶帽子没区别。 **Zhè liǎng dǐng màozi méi qūbié.**
There is no difference between these two hats.

→ 别动，让我看看。 **Bié dòng, ràng wǒ kànkan.**
Don't move, let me take a look.

| ` | ` | 广 | 疒 | 疒 | 疒 | 疒 | 病 |
| 病 | 病 | 病 | 病 | 病 | | | |

病

bìng   sickness, illness

疒 / 10 strokes

*His **sickness** made him cough a lot.*

病人	**bìngrén**	patient (in hospital)
病房	**bìngfáng**	ward (in hospital)
毛病	**máobìng**	fault, defect
病毒	**bìngdú**	virus

Chinese Characters Writing Practice Pad—**Character #156**

电	子	词	典	可	能	有	病	毒	。
好	，	那	先	杀	病	毒	。		

→ 电子词典可能有病毒。 **Diànzǐ cídiǎn kěnéng yǒu bìngdú.**
This electronic dictionary may have a virus.

→ 好，那先杀病毒。 **Hǎo, nà xiān shā bìngdú.**
Okay, let's kill the virus first.

丨	⼘	⼞	止	步	步	步	步
步	步						

步

bù   a step, a pace

止 / 7 strokes

*To stay healthy, it is recommended walking 10,000 **steps** a day.*

散步	**sànbù**	to go for a walk; leisurely walk
进步	**jìnbù**	to improve; progress
退步	**tuìbù**	to regress; regression
逐步	**zhúbù**	progressively, step by step

Chinese Characters Writing Practice Pad—**Character #157**

到公园去散步，好吗？

对不起，现在不行。

→ 到公园去散步，好吗？ **Dào gōngyuán qù sànbù, hǎo ma?**
Shall we go for a walk in the park?

→ 对不起，现在不行。 **Duìbuqǐ, xiànzài bùxíng.**
Sorry, I can't do it right now.

长　　　长　　　长　　　长　　　长　　　长　　　长

长

長
Traditional

Giraffes have **long** necks.

1. **cháng**　length; long
2. **zhǎng**　to grow; chief, head

长 / 4 strokes

长头发	**cháng tóufa**	long hair
长城	**Cháng Chéng**	the Great Wall
长江	**Cháng Jiāng**	Yangtze River
长期	**chángqī**	long term, long period of time
长处	**chángchù**	strong point
长大	**zhǎngdà**	to grow up

Chinese Characters Writing Practice Pad—**Character #158**

我 长 期 居 住 在 美 国 。

你 把 汉 语 都 忘 了 。

→ 我长期居住在美国。 **Wǒ chángqī jūzhù zài Měiguó.**
I have lived in the United States for a long time

→ 你把汉语都忘了。 **Nǐ bǎ Hànyǔ dōu wàng le.**
You forgot your Chinese.

| 丨 | 丩 | 丷 | 𱶧 | 㳠 | 常 | 常 | 常 |
| 常 | 常 | 常 | 常 | 常 | 常 | | |

常

cháng   always, ever, often

巾 / 11 strokes

*The family **always** goes to the library on Saturday.*

经常	**jīngcháng**	frequently, regularly
常常	**chángcháng**	always, ever, often
正常	**zhèngcháng**	regular, normal
平常	**píngcháng**	ordinary

Chinese Characters Writing Practice Pad—**Character #159**

他经常迟到。

那他应该早点儿睡觉。

→ 他经常迟到。 **Tā jīngcháng chídào.** He is always late.

→ 那他应该早点儿睡觉。 **Nà tā yīnggāi zǎodiǎnr shuìjiào.**
He should go to bed earlier.

一	圵	圵	场	场	场	场	场
场							

场

場
Traditional

We play soccer at
this **place**.

chǎng   location, place

土 / 6 strokes

足球场	**zúqiú chǎng**	football field
操场	**cāochǎng**	playground, sports field
广场	**guǎngchǎng**	public square, plaza
市场	**shìchǎng**	market

Chinese Characters Writing Practice Pad—**Character #160**

中	国	很	流	行	广	场	舞	。	
很	多	人	到	广	场	跳	舞	。	

→ 中国很流行广场舞。 **Zhōngguó hěn liúxíng guǎngchǎng wǔ.**
Public square dancing is very popular in China.

→ 很多人到广场跳舞。 **Hěn duō rén dào guǎngchǎng tiàowǔ.**
Lots of people gather to dance in public squares.

| 丨 | 口 | 口 | 叫 | 叩 | 唱 | 唱 | 唱 |

| 唱 | 唱 | 唱 | 唱 | 唱 | 唱 | | |

唱

chàng to sing

口 / 11 strokes

*Many people love to **sing** in a karaoke bar.*

唱歌	**chànggē**	to sing; singing
演唱	**yǎnchàng**	to sing for an audience
演唱会	**yǎnchànghuì**	vocal recital or concert
歌唱家	**gēchàngjiā**	singer

Chinese Characters Writing Practice Pad—**Character #161**

你	喜	欢	听	谁	的	演	唱	会	?
"	五	月	天	"	的	或	者	周	杰
伦	的	。							

→ 你喜欢听谁的演唱会？**Nǐ xǐhuan tīng shéi de yǎnchànghuì?** Whose concert do you like?

→ "五月天"的或者周杰伦的。**"Wǔyuè tiān" de huòzhě Zhōu Jiélún de.** May Day's or Jay Chou's.

凵	屮	屮	出	出	出	出	出

出

chū   to exit, to come out

凵 / 5 strokes

*He **came out** of the pool, shivering.*

出口	**chūkǒu**	exit
出现	**chūxiàn**	to appear, to emerge
出生	**chūshēng**	to be born
出发	**chūfā**	to set off

Chinese Characters Writing Practice Pad—**Character #162**

他	们	明	天	出	发	去	德	国	。
我	不	能	跟	他	们	一	起	去	。

→ 他们明天出发去德国。 **Tāmen míngtiān chūfā qù Déguó.**
They are departing for Germany tomorrow.

→ 我不能跟他们一起去。 **Wǒ bù néng gēn tāmen yìqǐ qù.**
I can't go with them.

` `	`丷`	`兰`	`半`	`弟`	`弟`	`弟`	弟
弟	弟						

弟

dì   younger brother

弓 / 7 strokes

*My **younger brother** wears glasses.*

弟弟	**dìdi**	younger brother
姐弟	**jiědì**	older sister and younger brother
兄弟	**xiōngdi**	brothers
徒弟	**túdi**	apprentice, disciple

Chinese Characters Writing Practice Pad—**Character #163**

你有兄弟姐妹吗？

我有三个弟弟。

→ 你有兄弟姐妹吗？ **Nǐ yǒu xiōngdì jiěmèi ma?**
Do you have any siblings?

→ 我有三个弟弟。 **Wǒ yǒu sān gè dìdi.**
I have three younger brothers.

| 乀 | 乆 | 女 | 女 | 女 | 女 | 妹 | 妹 |

| 妹 | 妹 | 妹 | | | | | |

妹

mèi　younger sister

女 / 8 strokes

*His **younger sister** learns ballet.*

小妹	**xiǎo mèi**	little sister
妹妹	**mèimei**	younger sister
表妹	**biǎomèi**	younger female cousin
兄妹	**xiōngmèi**	brothers and sisters

你妹妹今年几年级？

六年级了。

→ 你妹妹今年几年级？ **Nǐ mèimei jīnnián jǐ niánjí?**
Which grade is your younger sister in this year?

→ 六年级了。 **Liù niánjí le.** Grade 6.

㇓	犭	犭	犭	狗	狗	狗	狗
狗	狗	狗					

狗

gǒu　　dog

犭 / 8 strokes

*This **dog** can be a watch**dog**.*

小狗	**xiǎogǒu**	puppy
狗熊	**gǒuxióng**	black bear
搜狗	**sōugǒu**	Sougou search engine, www.sogou.com
遛狗	**liùgǒu**	to walk a dog

Chinese Characters Writing Practice Pad—**Character #165**

你去哪儿？

去遛狗。

→ 你去哪儿？ **Nǐ qù nǎr?** Where are you going?

→ 去遛狗。 **Qù liùgǒu.** Walk the dog.

刁	又	又	又勺	又勺	鸡	鸡	鸡
鸡	鸡						

鸡

雞
Traditional

The **chickens** were kept in coops.

jī   fowl, chicken

鸟 / 7 strokes

鸡蛋	**jīdàn**	chicken egg
鸡肉	**jīròu**	chicken meat
鸡汤	**jītāng**	chicken soup
鸡腿	**jītuǐ**	drumstick
炸鸡	**zhájī**	deep-fried chicken

Chinese Characters Writing Practice Pad—**Character #166**

我	不	喜	欢	吃	煎	鸡	蛋	。	
吃	煮	鸡	蛋	吗	？				

→ 我不喜欢吃煎鸡蛋。 **Wǒ bù xǐhuan chī jiān jīdàn.**
I don't like fried eggs.

→ 吃煮鸡蛋吗？ **Chī zhǔ jīdàn ma?** How about boiled eggs?

一 ナ 左 东 东 东 东 东

东
東
Traditional

dōng
一 / 5 strokes

east, host (i.e. sitting on the east side of the guest)

The sun rises in the **east** every morning.

东方	**dōngfāng**	east
东西	**dōngxi**	stuff, thing
东边	**dōngbian**	east side
东南亚	**Dōngnányà**	Southeast Asia

Chinese Characters Writing Practice Pad—**Character #167**

你	今	天	做	什	么	？			
去	买	东	西	。					

→ 你今天做什么？ **Nǐ jīntiān zuò shénme?**
What are you doing today?

→ 去买东西。 **Qù mǎi dōngxi.** I am going shopping.

您

nín you (courteous, formal)

心 / 11 strokes

"Good morning to **you,**" the bellboy greets the guest.

您好   **nínhǎo**   hello (polite)

您们   **nínmen**   you (plural)

请您回复   **qǐng nín huífù**   please reply

您好，您找谁？

王老师在吗？

→ 您好，您找谁？ **Nín hǎo, nín zhǎo shéi?**
Hello, whom are you looking for?

→ 王老师在吗？ **Wáng lǎoshi zài ma?** Is Teacher Wang in?

| 丿 | 刂 | ⺕ | ⺕ | 非 | 非 | 非 | 非 |
| 非 | 非 | 非 | | | | | |

非

fēi   to not be, not; wrong

非 / 8 strokes

*In some countries, it is **not** legal to buy guns.*

非常	**fēicháng**	very, very much; unusual
除非	**chúfēi**	unless, only when, only if
非法	**fēifǎ**	illegal
是非	**shìfēi**	right and wrong, quarrel

Chinese Characters Writing Practice Pad—**Character #169**

你	喜	欢	打	网	球	吗	？		
非	常	喜	欢	。					

→ 你喜欢打网球吗？ **Nǐ xǐhuan dǎ wǎngqiú ma?**
Do you like to play tennis?

→ 非常喜欢。 **Fēicháng xǐhuan.** Very much.

| 乛 | 一 | 帀 | 襾 | 襾 | 西 | 覀 | 要 |

| 要 | 要 | 要 | 要 | | | | |

要

1. **yāo**   to demand, to request
2. **yào**   important, vital; to want

^西 / 9 strokes

"*I demand to see your manager at once.*"

I demand....

想要	**xiǎngyào**	to want to, to feel like
需要	**xūyào**	need to; a need
要求	**yāoqiú**	to request; a request
重要	**zhòngyào**	main, significant, important
主要	**zhǔyào**	main, chief

Chinese Characters Writing Practice Pad—**Character #170**

我 去 买 东 西 ， 你 要 什 么
？

帮 我 买 一 个 水 杯 吧 。

→ 我去买东西，你要什么？ **Wǒ qù mǎi dōngxi, nǐ yào shénme?** I am going to shop. Do you need anything?

→ 帮我买一个水杯吧。 **Bāng wǒ mǎi yí gè shuǐbēi ba.** Help me get a glass.

一 ナ 左 左 左 左 左 左

左

zuǒ left

工 / 5 strokes

*He writes with his **left** hand.*

左脚	**zuǒ jiǎo**	left foot
左转	**zuǒzhuǎn**	to turn left
左面	**zuǒmian**	left side
左右	**zuǒyòu**	about; the left and right sides

Chinese Characters Writing Practice Pad—**Character #171**

你 想 买 多 少 本 书 ？

五 十 本 左 右 。

→ 你想买多少本书？ **Nǐ xiǎng mǎi duōshao běn shū?**
How many books do you want to buy?

→ 五十本左右。 **Wǔshí běn zuǒyòu.** About fifty books.

ノ	ᄂ	ᄃ	勹	匂	每	每	每
每	每						

每

měi　　each, every

母 / 7 strokes

EVERY DROP
COUNTS!

Every drop of water counts.
Water is precious.

每天	**měitiān**	every day
每次	**měicì**	every time
每人	**měirén**	each person, everybody
每处	**měichù**	everywhere, anywhere

Chinese Characters Writing Practice Pad—**Character #172**

每	天	都	要	做	运	动	。		
每	次	做	多	长	时	间	？		

→ 每天都要做运动。 **Měitiān dōu yào zuò yùndòng.**
You should exercise every day.

→ 每次做多长时间？ **Měicì zuò duōcháng shíjiān?**
How long each time?

动 | 动 | 勾 | 云 | 云 | 三 | 二

动

动
動
Traditional

dòng   to move

力 / 6 strokes

Exercises help to move our body so they are good.

运动	**yùndòng**	exercise, sports, campaign
动物	**dòngwù**	animals
动物园	**dòngwùyuán**	zoo
动作	**dòngzuò**	movement, action

Chinese Characters Writing Practice Pad—**Character #173**

多做运动身体好。

没错。

→ 多做运动身体好。 **Duō zuò yùndòng shēntǐ hǎo.**
More exercise is good for the body.

→ 没错。 **Méi cuò.** Right.

| ゛ | 宀 | 广 | 庁 | 庄 | 庆 | 床 | 床 |

| 床 | 床 | | | | | | |

床

chuáng   bed

广 / 7 strokes

*This **bed** has a mosquito net.*

起床	**qǐchuáng**	to get up of bed
床单	**chuángdān**	bedsheet
单人床	**dānrén chuáng**	single bed
床铺	**chuángpù**	bed

Chinese Characters Writing Practice Pad—**Character #174**

你 每 天 几 点 起 床 ?

我 每 天 七 点 半 起 床 。

→ 你每天几点起床？ **Nǐ měitiān jǐ diǎn qǐchuáng?**
When do you get up every day?

→ 我每天都七点半起床。 **Wǒ měitiān dōu qī diǎn bàn qǐchuáng.** I get up at 7:30 every day.

ㄧ	ㄇ	ㅁ	虫	虫	串	串	贵

贵	贵	贵	贵				

贵

贵
Traditional

guì
贝 / 9 strokes

expensive, noble,
precious

*This rare vase is
very **expensive**.*

太贵了	**tài guì le**	too expensive
昂贵	**ángguì**	expensive, costly
宝贵	**bǎoguì**	valuable, precious
珍贵	**zhēnguì**	rare and precious

Chinese Characters Writing Practice Pad—**Character #175**

这个手机五千块。

太贵了！

→ 这个手机五千块。 **Zhè ge shǒujī wǔqiān kuài.**
This cellphone costs $5000.

→ 太贵了！ **Tài guì le.** It is too expensive.

| 一 | 寸 | 寸 | 寸 | 讨 | 过 | 过 | 过 |
| 过 | | | | | | | |

过

過
Traditional

guò
辶 / 6 strokes

to cross, to go over,
to pass (time)

*We use this to **cross over** to the island.*

难过	**nánguò**	to feel sad, to feel bad
不过	**búguò**	no more than; but
超过	**chāoguò**	to surpass, to exceed
过程	**guòchéng**	course of events, process

Chinese Characters Writing Practice Pad—**Character #176**

別难过了。

我没事，谢谢。

→ 别难过了。 **Bié nánguò le.** Don't be sad.
→ 我没事，谢谢。 **Wǒ méi shì, xièxie.** I am ok, thank you.

纟	纟	纟	纟	纟	红	红	红
红							

红

红
Traditional

hóng   red, popular

纟 / 6 strokes

*Children are most happy to receive **red** packets on Chinese New Year.*

红花	**hónghuā**	safflower
红酒	**hóngjiǔ**	red wine
红包	**hóngbāo**	red packet (with money)
走红	**zǒuhóng**	to become popular

Chinese Characters Writing Practice Pad—**Character #177**

法	国	的	红	酒	最	有	名	。	
我	很	喜	欢	喝	。				

→ 法国的红酒最有名。 **Fǎguó de hóngjiǔ zuì yǒumíng.**
The French red wine is the most famous.

→ 我很喜欢喝。 **Wǒ hěn xǐhuan hē.**
I like to drink it very much.

从　　人　　从　　从　　从　　从　　从

从　　從
Traditional

cóng　　from, through, via

人 / 4 strokes

*The little children learn to go **through** the tunnel.*

从不	**cóngbù**	never
从…到…	**cóng…dào…**	from… to…
从来	**cónglái**	always, at all times
从头	**cóngtóu**	from the start
自从	**zìcóng**	since (a time), ever since

Chinese Characters Writing Practice Pad—**Character #178**

从	香	港	到	北	京	要	多	久	？
坐	火	车	要	2	4	小	时	。	

→ 从香港到北京要多久？ **Cóng Xiānggǎng dào Běijīng yào duō jiǔ?** How long does it take to go from Hong Kong to Beijing?

→ 坐火车要24小时。 **Zuò huǒchē yào 24 xiǎoshí.** It takes 24 hours by train.

| 𠂉 | ⺮ | ⺮ | ⺮ | ⺮ | ⺮ | 笁 | 笁 |
| 笙 | 笁 | 等 | 等 | 等 | 等 | 等 | |

等

děng

⺮ / 12 strokes

to wait for; class;
equal to, same as

The schoolboy **waited**
at the gate for his mom.

等一下	**děng yíxià**	to wait a moment, later
等不及	**děng bùjí**	can't wait
头等	**tóuděng**	first class
等于	**děngyú**	to equal

Chinese Characters Writing Practice Pad—**Character #179**

请问，我现在可以上车

吗？

请等一下。

→ 请问，我现在可以上车吗？ **Qǐngwèn, wǒ xiànzài kěyǐ shàng chē ma?** Excuse me, can I get on the bus now?

→ 请等一下。 **Qǐng děng yíxià.** Just a moment.

𠂉	𫠆	𠂊	𫐀	鱼	角	鱼	鱼
鱼	鱼	鱼					

鱼

魚
Traditional

yú　fish

鱼 / 8 strokes

The man caught
a big **fish**.

钓鱼	**diàoyú**	to fish (with line and hook)
金鱼	**jīnyú**	goldfish
鲸鱼	**jīngyú**	whale
炸鱼	**zháyú**	deep-fried fish

Chinese Characters Writing Practice Pad—**Character #180**

爸爸 很 喜 欢 钓 鱼 。

你 学 会 钓 鱼 了 吗 ？

→ 爸爸很喜欢钓鱼。 **Bàba hěn xǐhuan diàoyú.**
My father likes fishing very much.

→ 你学会钓鱼了吗？ **Nǐ xuéhuì diàoyú le ma?**
Have you learned how to fish?

一	十	土	步	考	考	考	考
考							

考

kǎo

老 / 6 strokes

to check, to verify, to test, to examine

*The eye doctor **tested** my eyesight yesterday.*

考试	**kǎoshì**	to take an exam; exam
考虑	**kǎolǜ**	to consider; consideration
考证	**kǎozhèng**	to validate
参考	**cānkǎo**	to refer; reference

Chinese Characters Writing Practice Pad—**Character #181**

我	不	喜	欢	考	试	。			
我	也	不	喜	欢	。				

→ 我不喜欢考试。 **Wǒ bù xǐhuan kǎoshì.** I don't like exams.

→ 我也不喜欢。 **Wǒ yě bù xǐhuan.** Neither do I.

㇀	⼆	卡	井	讠井	讲	进	进
进	进						

进 進
Traditional

jìn
辶 / 7 strokes

to go forward,
to advance, to go in

*The schoolboy was
asked to go in by
the principal.*

进来	**jìnlái**	to come in
进行	**jìnxíng**	to conduct; in progress
促进	**cùjìn**	to advance
进步	**jìnbù**	to improve; improvement

Chinese Characters Writing Practice Pad—**Character #182**

我	可	以	进	来	吗	？			
请	进	。							

→ 我可以进来吗？ **Wǒ kěyǐ jìnlái ma?** May I come in?

→ 请进。 **Qǐngjìn.** Come in please.

乚	幺	纟	纟	纟	经	经	经
经	经	经					

经

经
Traditional

jīng
纟 / 8 strokes

to pass through;
classics, scripture

A lot of people like to quote scriptures.

经过	**jīngguò**	to pass, to go through; process
圣经	**Shèngjīng**	Bible
经理	**jīnglǐ**	manager, director
经济	**jīngjì**	economy, economics
经验	**jīngyàn**	experience (n. & v.)

Chinese Characters Writing Practice Pad—**Character #183**

喂，请问林经理在吗？

我是，你是谁？

→ 喂，请问林经理在吗？ **Wéi, qǐngwèn Lín jīnglǐ zài ma?**
Hello, may I speak to manager Lin?

→ 我是，你是谁？ **Wǒ shì, nǐ shì shéi?**
Speaking, who are you?

`	` `	氵	氵	汸	汸	汸	汸
浐	游	游	游	游	游	游	

游

遊 (only for "walk" & "tour" meanings)
Traditional

yóu
氵 / 12 strokes

to walk, to tour,
to travel, to swim

*We love **traveling** and taking photos.*

旅游	**lǚyóu**	trip, tourism
电子游戏	**diànzǐ yóuxì**	electronic games
导游	**dǎoyóu**	tour guide
游泳	**yóuyǒng**	to swim; swimming

Chinese Characters Writing Practice Pad—**Character #184**

我	喜	欢	玩	电	子	游	戏	。	
我	们	一	起	玩	。				

→ 我喜欢玩电子游戏。 **Wǒ xǐhuan wán diànzǐ yóuxì.**
I love playing electronic games.

→ 我们一起玩。 **Wǒmen yìqǐ wán.** Let's play together.

汽

qì   steam, vapor

氵 / 7 strokes

*When the water boils, **steam** escapes from the kettle.*

汽油   **qìyóu**   gasoline
汽水   **qìshuǐ**   soft drinks, fizzy water
汽车   **qìchē**   motorcar
汽艇   **qìtǐng**   motorboat

Chinese Characters Writing Practice Pad—**Character #185**

我真的很喜欢喝汽水。

你不能每天都喝。

→ 我真的很喜欢喝汽水。 **Wǒ zhēn de hěn xǐhuan hē qìshuǐ.**
I really like soft drinks.

→ 你不能每天都喝。 **Nǐ bù néng měitiān dōu hē.**
You can't drink them every day.

`	讠	讠	讠	讠	讠	误	课
课	课	课	课	课			

课

課
Traditional

kè
讠 / 10 strokes

subject, course, lesson

	Tuesday	
8:30	Assembly	
9:00	Maths	
11:00	English	

*My math **lesson** is at 9.00.*

数学课	**shùxué kè**	math class
下课	**xiàkè**	to finish class
功课	**gōngkè**	homework
课程	**kèchéng**	curriculum

Chinese Characters Writing Practice Pad—**Character #186**

你喜欢什么课？

体育课。

→ 你喜欢什么课？ **Nǐ xǐhuan shénme kè?**
Which class do you like?

→ 体育课。 **Tǐyù kè.** I like Physical Education class.

早　早

早

早

zǎo   early, morning

日 / 6 strokes

*Early in the **morning**, we were awakened by the cockerel.*

早上	**zǎoshang**	early morning
早饭	**zǎofàn**	breakfast
迟早	**chízǎo**	sooner or later
最早	**zuìzǎo**	earliest

Chinese Characters Writing Practice Pad—**Character #187**

書 最 早 周 三 可 以 寄 到。

没 问 题, 多 少 钱 ?

→ 书最早周三可以寄到。 **Shū zuìzǎo zhōu sān kěyǐ jì dào.**
The earliest delivery date of the books is Wednesday.

→ 没问题, 多少钱 ? **Méi wèntí, duōshao qián?**
No problem, how much is the delivery?

`丶` `丶丿` `丷` 火 火 火 火

火

huǒ fire; angry

火 / 4 strokes

*The **fire** kept us warm when it was cold at night.*

火车站	**huǒchēzhàn**	train station
火锅	**huǒguō**	hotpot
火鸡	**huǒjī**	turkey
火柴	**huǒchái**	match (for lighting a fire)
发火	**fāhuǒ**	angry

Chinese Characters Writing Practice Pad—**Character #188**

我	们	在	哪	儿	见	面	?		
五	点	十	分	火	车	站	见	。	

→ 我们在哪儿见面？ **Wǒmen zài nǎr jiànmiàn?**
Where shall we meet?

→ 五点十分火车站见。 **Wǔ diǎn shí fēn huǒchēzhàn jiàn.**
5:10 at the train station.

✓	八	公	公	公	公	公

公

gōng   public, collectively
八 / 4 strokes   owned, common

*The **public** bus is cheap and easy to use.*

公共汽车	**gōnggòng qìchē**	bus
公布	**gōngbù**	to announce, to make public
公斤	**gōngjīn**	kilogram
公园	**gōngyuán**	park

Chinese Characters Writing Practice Pad—**Character #189**

我 想 去 博 物 馆。

坐 3 5 路 公 共 汽 车。

→ 我想去博物馆。 **Wǒ xiǎng qù bówùguǎn.**
  I would like to go to the museum.

→ 坐35路公共汽车。 **Zuò 35 lù gōnggòng qìchē.**
  Take bus No. 35.

| 亻 | 彳 | 彳 | 彳 | 彳 | 得 | 得 | 得 |
| 得 | 得 | 得 | 得 | 得 | 得 | | |

得

*He **must** reach the airport by 10.30 PM.*

1. **de** structural particle, used after a verb
2. **dé** to obtain, to get
3. **děi** have to, must, ought to, need to

彳 / 11 strokes

跑得快	**pǎo de kuài**	to be able to run quickly
觉得	**juéde**	to think, to feel
获得	**huòdé**	to obtain, to receive
不得不	**bù dé bù**	have to, have no choice

Chinese Characters Writing Practice Pad—**Character #190**

我 觉 得 特 别 冷 。

你 得 把 空 调 关 上 。

→ 我觉得特别冷。 **Wǒ juéde tèbié lěng.** I feel cold.

→ 你得把空调关上。 **Nǐ děi bǎ kōngtiáo guānshàng.**
  You must turn off the air conditioning.

次

cì

欠 / 6 strokes

next in sequence, time

Annie

*Annie is **next** in line to buy the tickets for the show.*

一次	**yí cì**	one time
其次	**qícì**	next, secondly
层次	**céngcì**	layer, level
次要	**cìyào**	secondary

Chinese Characters Writing Practice Pad—**Character #191**

我	去	过	一	次	美	国	。		
我	没	去	过	。					

→ 我去过一次美国。 **Wǒ qù guò yí cì Měiguó.**
I have been to the US once.

→ 我没去过。 **Wǒ méi qù guò.** I have not been to the US.

| 忄 | 忄 | 忄 | 忄 | 忄 | 忄 | 忄 | 懂 |
| 懂 | 懂 | 懂 | 懂 | 懂 | 懂 | 懂 | 懂 |

懂

dǒng

忄 / 15 strokes

to understand,
to comprehend

Little James
understands *when his*
mom speaks to him.

不懂	**bùdǒng**	do not understand
懂不懂	**dǒng bu dǒng**	understand or not
懂事	**dǒngshì**	sensible, thoughtful, intelligent
懂得	**dǒngdé**	to understand, to know

Chinese Characters Writing Practice Pad—**Character #192**

你	懂	中	文	吗	?				
能	看	懂	一	点	儿	。			

→ 你懂中文吗？ **Nǐ dǒng Zhōngwén ma?**
Do you know Chinese?

→ 能看懂一点儿。 **Néng kàn dǒng yìdiǎnr.**
I can read a little bit.

| 一 | ナ | 艹 | 共 | 共 | 共 | 共 | 共 |
| 共 | | | | | | | |

共

gòng

八 / 6 strokes

to share, common, general

*This is a **common** meeting space for the employees.*

一共	**yígòng**	total, altogether
共同	**gòngtóng**	common, joint; jointly
总共	**zǒnggòng**	altogether, in sum, in all
共和国	**gònghéguó**	republic (style of government)

Chinese Characters Writing Practice Pad—**Character #193**

你	们	多	少	人	去	旅	行	？
总	共	二	十	人	。			

→ 你们多少人去旅行？ **Nǐmen duōshao rén qù lǚxíng?**
How many of you are going to travel?

→ 总共二十人。 **Zǒnggòng èrshí rén.** Twenty in total.

| 阝 | 阝 | 阴 | 阴 | 阴 | 阴 | 阴 | 阴 |
| 阴 | | | | | | | |

阴 陰
Traditional

yīn   yin, dark, secretive
阝 / 6 strokes

*The day turned **dark** suddenly.*

阴天	**yīntiān**	cloudy day
阴雨	**yīnyǔ**	cloudy and rainy
阴历	**yīnlì**	lunar calendar
阴谋	**yīnmóu**	conspiracy, plot

Chinese Characters Writing Practice Pad—**Character #194**

明天阴天。

阴天适合远足。

→ 明天阴天。 **Míngtiān yīntiān.** Tomorrow will be cloudy.

→ 阴天适合远足。 **Yīntiān shìhé yuǎnzú.**
Cloudy days are good for hiking.

| ⺌ | 八 | 忄 | 忄 | 忆 | 快 | 快 | 快 |
| 快 | 快 | | | | | | |

快

kuài rapid, quick, fast

忄 / 7 strokes

*The subway is very **fast**.*

快餐	**kuàicān**	fast food
快乐	**kuàilè**	happy, merry
凉快	**liángkuai**	cool, pleasantly cool
愉快	**yúkuài**	cheerful, delightful

Chinese Characters Writing Practice Pad—**Character #195**

北	方	的	夏	天	很	凉	快	。	
那	我	们	明	年	暑	假	去	北	方
。									

→ 北方的夏天很凉快。**Běifāng de xiàtiān hěn liángkuai.**
The summer in the north is cool.

→ 那我们明年暑假去北方。**Nà wǒmen míngnián shǔjià qù běifāng.** Then we will go to the north next summer.

房

fáng house, room

戶 / 8 strokes

*The **room** is spacious.*

房子	**fángzi**	house, apartment
房间	**fángjiān**	room
厨房	**chúfáng**	kitchen
房东	**fángdōng**	landlord

Chinese Characters Writing Practice Pad—**Character #196**

哪	个	是	我	的	房	间	？		
你	的	房	间	在	楼	下	。		

→ 哪个是我的房间？ **Nǎge shì wǒ de fángjiān?**
Which is my room?

→ 你的房间在楼下。 **Nǐ de fángjiān zài lóu xià.**
Your room is downstairs.

| 一 | 十 | 圡 | 走 | 走 | 走 | 走 | 走 |
| 走 | 走 | | | | | | |

走

zǒu   to walk, to go,
走 / 7 strokes   to run

Please **walk** the dog
every evening.

走进   **zǒujìn**   to enter
走过   **zǒuguò**   to walk past
带走   **dàizǒu**   to take away
走廊   **zǒuláng**   corridor

Chinese Characters Writing Practice Pad—**Character #197**

洗手间在哪儿？

穿过走廊就看到了。

→ 洗手间在哪儿？ **Xǐshǒujiān zài nǎr?**
Where is the washroom?

→ 穿过走廊就看到了。 **Chuānguò zǒuláng jiù kàn dào le.**
You'll see it after you go past the corridor.

⼀	⼆	元	元	元	远	远	远
远	远						

远 遠
Traditional

yuǎn far, distant, remote

辶 / 7 strokes

*This village is **remote** and there is little transportation.*

永远	**yǒngyuǎn**	forever, eternal
望远镜	**wàngyuǎnjìng**	binoculars, telescope
遥远	**yáoyuǎn**	distant, remote
远近闻名	**yuǎnjìn wénmíng**	well-known, famous

Chinese Characters Writing Practice Pad—**Character #198**

这个餐馆远近闻名。

那我们一定要去。

→ 这个餐馆远近闻名。 **Zhège cānguǎn yuǎnjìn wénmíng.**
The restaurant is well-known.

→ 那我们一定要去。 **Nà wǒmen yídìng yào qù.**
In that case, we should give it a try.

一 一 厅 两 两 两 两 两

两 两

两
两
Traditional

liǎng   two, both; weight
一 / 7 strokes   of about 50 grams

Both items weigh
about the same.

两个人   **liǎng gè rén**   two people
一两肉   **yì liǎng ròu**   50 grams of meat
两旁   **liǎngpáng**   both sides, either side
一举两得   **yìjǔ-liǎngdé**   one move, two gains; kill
                two birds with one stone

Chinese Characters Writing Practice Pad—**Character #199**

房子的两旁有很多树。

都是松树。

→ 房子的两旁有很多树。**Fángzi de liǎngpáng yǒu hěn duō shù.** There are many trees on both sides of the house.

→ 都是松树。**Dōu shì sōngshù.** They are all pine trees.

二	耂	耂	耂	耂	孝	孝	孝
孝	教	教	教	教	教		

教

1. **jiào** to teach; religion, teaching
2. **jiāo** teaching; to instruct

攵 / 11 strokes

*Father **teaches** my brother how to ride a bike.*

教室	**jiàoshì**	classroom
教育	**jiàoyù**	to educate, to teach; education
教练	**jiàoliàn**	coach
佛教	**Fójiào**	Buddhism
教课	**jiāokè**	to teach a class, to lecture

Chinese Characters Writing Practice Pad—**Character #200**

游泳教练很严格。

对！。

→ 游泳教练很严格。 **Yóuyǒng jiàoliàn hěn yángé.**
The coach for swimming is very strict.

→ 对！ **Duì.** Right.

男

nán   male

田 / 7 strokes

TOILET

*The sign says the toilet is for **males**.*

男人	**nánren**	man, male
男孩	**nánhái**	boy
男性	**nánxìng**	the male sex
男老师	**nán lǎoshī**	male teacher

Chinese Characters Writing Practice Pad—**Character #201**

幼儿园需要男老师。

我同意。

→ 幼儿园需要男老师。**Yòu'éryuán xūyào nán lǎoshī.**
Kindergartens need male teachers.

→ 我同意。**Wǒ tóngyì.** I agree.

| 一 | 十 | 扌 | 扩 | 找 | 找 | 找 | 找 |
| 找 | 找 | | | | | | |

找

zhǎo   to find, to look for

扌 / 7 strokes

"Help me. I'm **looking for** my glasses."

找人	**zhǎorén**	to look for someone
找钱	**zhǎoqián**	to give change
寻找	**xúnzhǎo**	to seek, to look for
找到	**zhǎodào**	to have found

Chinese Characters Writing Practice Pad—**Character #202**

你 找 到 邮 局 了 吗 ？

找 到 了 。

→ 你找到邮局了吗？ **Nǐ zhǎodào yóujú le ma?**
  Did you find the post office?
→ 找到了。 **Zhǎodào le.** Yes, I found it.

| 忄 | 八 | 忄 | 忄 | 忄曰 | 忄曰 | 忄曰 | 忄曰 |
| 慢 | 慢 | 慢 | 慢 | 慢 | 慢 | 慢 | 慢 |

慢

màn　slow

忄 / 14 strokes

A snail moves **slowly**.

慢跑	**mànpǎo**	jogging; to jog
慢慢地	**mànmàn de**	slowly, unhurriedly
缓慢	**huǎnmàn**	slow, slow-moving
慢车	**mànchē**	slow train with many stops

Chinese Characters Writing Practice Pad—**Character #203**

慢	车	的	车	票	比	较	便	宜	。
我	买	两	张	。					

→ 慢车的车票比较便宜。 **Mànchē de chēpiào bǐjiào piányi.**
The tickets for slow trains are cheaper.

→ 我买两张。 **Wǒ mǎi liǎng zhāng.** I will buy two tickets.

| 一 | 丁 | 丂 | 可 | 叮 | 哥 | 哥 | 哥 |
| 哥 | 哥 | 哥 | 哥 | 哥 | | | |

哥

gē   older brother

口 / 10 strokes

*My **older brother**
looks stern but he
is not really so.*

哥哥	**gēgē**	older brother
大哥	**dàgē**	eldest brother
哥们	**gēmen**	brothers, buddies
帅哥	**shuàigē**	handsome guy

Chinese Characters Writing Practice Pad—**Character #204**

	你	大	哥	比	较	矮	。			
	在	家	里	我	最	高	。			

→ 你大哥比较矮。 **Nǐ dàgē bǐjiào ǎi.**
Your eldest brother is short.

→ 在家里我最高。 **Zài jiā li wǒ zuì gāo.**
I am the tallest in the family.

| 丿 | 冂 | 曰 | 田 | 甲 | 里 | 累 | 累 |

| 累 | 累 | 累 | 累 | 累 | 累 | | |

累

1. **lèi** tired, weary; to strain
2. **lěi** to accumulate

糸 / 11 strokes

*Little by little, the savings **accumulate** to a few hundred dollars.*

积累	**jīlěi**	to accumulate; accumulation
劳累	**láolèi**	tired, exhausted
累计	**lěijì**	to accumulate; cumulative
日积月累	**rìjīyuèlěi**	to accumulate over a long period of time

Chinese Characters Writing Practice Pad—**Character #205**

别	太	劳	累	了	。				
好	的	，	谢	谢	。				

→ 别太劳累了。 **Bié tài láolèi le.** Don't get too tired.

→ 好的，谢谢。 **Hǎode, xièxie.** Ok, thanks.

一	丁	后	可	可	可	可	可

可

kě   to approve; can,
口 / 5 strokes   may, able to

*A green light means
the cars **can** move.*

可以	**kěyǐ**	can; possible
可是	**kěshì**	but, however
可惜	**kěxī**	it is a pity; unfortunately
可怜	**kělián**	pitiful, pathetic; to have pity on

Chinese Characters Writing Practice Pad—**Character #206**

真可惜，没见到你。

没关系，下个月再见。

→ 真可惜，没见到你。 **Zhēn kěxī, méi jiàn dào nǐ.**
It's a pity that I didn't see you.

→ 没关系，下个月再见。 **Méiguānxi, xià gè yuè zàijiàn.** No problem, see you next month.

Copyright © 2022 Periplus Editions (HK) Ltd

㇑	㇃	忄	忄	忙	忙	忙	忙
忙							

忙

máng   to hurry, to rush;
忄 / 6 strokes   busy, hurriedly

*We see **busy** bees at work every morning.*

赶忙	**gǎnmáng**	to hurry, to hasten
匆忙	**cōngmáng**	hasty, hurried
急忙	**jímáng**	hastily
连忙	**liánmáng**	promptly, at once
很忙	**hěn máng**	very busy

Chinese Characters Writing Practice Pad—**Character #207**

你	走	得	太	匆	忙	了	。		
对	，	忘	了	带	手	机	。		

→ 你走得太匆忙了。 **Nǐzǒu de tài cōngmáng le.**
You left in a hurry.

→ 对，忘了带手机。 **Duì, wàng le dài shǒujī.**
Yes, I forgot to take the phone.

レ	ロ	ロ	足	足	足	足	足
跁	跁	跁	跑	跑	跑	跑	

跑

pǎo to run, to run away,
足 / 12 strokes to escape

The thief ran away, after snatching the handbag.

跑步	**pǎobù**	to run, to jog
跑车	**pǎochē**	racing car
跑道	**pǎodào**	athletic track, race track, runway
跑题	**pǎotí**	to digress, to stray from the topic
赛跑	**sàipǎo**	race (running); to race (running)

Chinese Characters Writing Practice Pad—**Character #208**

跑	步	可	以	减	肥	。			
我	不	想	减	肥	。				

→ 跑步可以减肥。 **Pǎobù kěyǐ jiǎnféi.**
Running will help to lose weight.

→ 我不想减肥。 **Wǒ bù xiǎng jiǎnféi.**
I don't want to lose weight.

| 丶 | 亠 | 亠 | 亠 | 离 | 离 | 离 | 离 |

| 离 | 离 | 离 | 离 | 离 | | | |

离

离
lí
亠 / 10 strokes

離
Traditional

to leave, to part from,
to be away from

*The young man **leaves**
his village to look for a
job in the city.*

离开	**líkāi**	to depart, to leave
距离	**jùlí**	distance
离婚	**líhūn**	to divorce; divorce
分离	**fēnlí**	to separate; separation

Chinese Characters Writing Practice Pad—**Character #209**

为	什	么	你	要	离	开	这	里	？
因	为	我	不	喜	欢	这	里	。	

→ 为什么你要离开这里？ **Wèishénme nǐ yào líkāi zhèlǐ?**
Why do you want to leave this place?

→ 因为我不喜欢这里。 **Yīnwèi wǒ bù xǐhuan zhèlǐ.**
Because I don't like it here.

丨	冂	月	日	日⼀	日⼆	日⼿	晴
晴	晴	晴	晴	晴	晴	晴	

晴

qíng   clear, fine (weather)

日 / 12 strokes

*On **clear** days tourists in hot air balloons can be seen.*

晴天	**qíngtiān**	clear sky, sunny day
晴雨表	**qíngyǔbiǎo**	barometer
晴朗	**qínglǎng**	sunny and cloudless
雨过天晴	**yǔguòtiānqíng**	literally, the sky clears after rain → new hopes after a disastrous period (idom)

Chinese Characters Writing Practice Pad—**Character #210**

天	空	晴	朗	。					
我	们	去	爬	山	好	吗	？		

→ 天空晴朗。 **Tiānkōng qínglǎng.** The sky is clear.

→ 我们去爬山好吗？ **Wǒmen qù pá shān hǎo ma?**
 Shall we go mountain climbing?

| 乛 | 劸 | 也 | 也 | 也 | 也 | | |

也

yě   also, too

乙 / 3 strokes

*This clock is old, and broken **too**.*

也是	**yěshì**	also
也许	**yěxǔ**	perhaps, maybe
也就是	**yějiùshì**	that is
再也	**zàiyě**	(not) any more

Chinese Characters Writing Practice Pad—**Character #211**

也	许	今	天	会	下	大	雨	。	
那	我	不	出	去	了	。			

→ 也许今天会下大雨。 **Yěxǔ jīntiān huì xià dàyǔ.**
Maybe it will rain heavily today.

→ 那我不出去了。 **Nà wǒ bù chūqù le.** Then I won't go out.

亅	冂	内	内	肉	肉	肉	肉
肉							

肉

ròu   meat, flesh

*I like to eat **meat**.*

冂 / 6 strokes

猪肉	**zhūròu**	pork
牛肉	**niúròu**	beef
烤肉	**kǎoròu**	barbecued meat
肉丸	**ròuwán**	meatball

Chinese Characters Writing Practice Pad—**Character #212**

猪 肉 的 价 钱 比 牛 肉 便 宜

得 多 。

那 羊 肉 呢 ？

→ 猪肉的价钱比牛肉便宜得多。 **Zhūròu de jiàqián bǐ niúròu piányi de duō.** The price of pork is much cheaper than that of beef.

→ 那羊肉呢？ **Nà yángròu ne?** What about lamb?

丶	丷	宀	宀	宐	宎	窂	窐
室	室	室	室				

室

shì   room, work unit

宀 / 9 strokes

*This is my **work unit**.*

室外	**shìwài**	outdoor
浴室	**yùshì**	bathing room
卧室	**wòshì**	bedroom
室友	**shìyǒu**	roommate, flat mate

Chinese Characters Writing Practice Pad—**Character #213**

你	的	中	文	讲	得	很	流	利	。
我	每	天	都	和	室	友	练	习	。

→ 你的中文讲得很流利。 **Nǐ de Zhōngwén jiǎng de hěn liúlì.**
You speak Chinese very fluently.

→ 我每天都和室友练习。 **Wǒ měitiān dōu hé shìyǒu liànxí.**
I practice Chinese with my roommates every day.

丁	刁	刁	司	司	司	司	司

司

SĪ
口 / 5 strokes

to take charge of, to manage; department

*My aunt **takes charge** of washing the clothes in her house.*

公司　　**gōngsī**　　(business) company, company

上司　　**shàngsī**　　boss, superior

司令　　**sīlìng**　　commanding officer

打官司　**dǎguānsi**　to file a lawsuit, to sue

Chinese Characters Writing Practice Pad—**Character #214**

这	是	一	家	上	市	公	司	。	
在	北	京	很	有	名	。			

→ 这是一家上市公司。 **Zhè shì yì jiā shàngshì gōngsī.**
  This is a listed company.

→ 在北京很有名。 **Zài Běijīng hěn yǒumíng.**
  It is very famous in Beijing.

丿	亻	仁	什	付	休	体	体
体	体						

体

體
Traditional

tǐ

亻 / 7 strokes

body, form, style, system

She keeps her body in good form by exercising.

身体	**shēntǐ**	body
体育	**tǐyù**	sports, physical education
集体	**jítǐ**	collective, team
具体	**jùtǐ**	concrete, definite, specific
体检	**tǐjiǎn**	medical examination

Chinese Characters Writing Practice Pad—**Character #215**

酒店的具体位置在哪？

你上网查查。

→ 酒店的具体位置在哪？ **Jiǔdiàn de jùtǐ wèizhi zài nǎ?**
Where is the exact location of the hotel?

→ 你上网查查。 **Nǐ shàngwǎng chácha.**
You can search on the Internet.

| ` | 丷 | 宀 | 宁 | 宫 | 宇 | 完 | 完 |

完

wán to finish, to be over

宀 / 7 strokes

*The game **is over** when there are no more moves.*

完成	**wánchéng**	to complete, to accomplish
完全	**wánquán**	complete, entire
完美	**wánměi**	perfect; perfection
完整	**wánzhěng**	complete, intact

Chinese Characters Writing Practice Pad—**Character #216**

他	的	体	操	动	作	很	完	美	。
去	年	他	拿	了	冠	军	。		

→ 他的体操动作很完美。 **Tā de tǐcāo dòngzuò hěn wánměi.**
His gymnastic movements are perfect.

→ 去年他拿了冠军。 **Qùnián tā ná le guànjūn.**
He was the champion last year.

| 丿 | 刀 | 月 | 日 | 日′ | 日″ | 日″ | 日″ |
| 日″ | 映 | 晚 | 晚 | 晚 | 晚 | | |

晚

wǎn   evening, night; late

日 / 11 strokes

*They have a **late** dinner.*

晚上	**wǎnshang**	evening, night
晚会	**wǎnhuì**	evening party
晚饭	**wǎnfàn**	dinner, evening meal
晚安	**wǎn'ān**	good night
太晚了	**tài wǎn le**	It's too late

Chinese Characters Writing Practice Pad—**Character #217**

晚	饭	不	要	吃	得	太	饱	。	
知	道	了	。						

→ 晚饭不要吃得太饱。 **Wǎnfàn búyào chī de tài bǎo.**
Don't eat too much for dinner.

→ 知道了。 **Zhīdào le.** OK, I know.

⼁	⼃	彳	彳	彳	往	往	往
往	往	往					

往

wǎng   to go (in a direction);
彳 / 8 strokes   to, towards

*The boy moves **towards** the car.*

往往	**wǎngwǎng**	often, frequently
交往	**jiāowǎng**	relationship; to be in contact with
往来	**wǎnglái**	dealings, contacts
往后	**wǎnghòu**	from now on, in the future
往返	**wǎngfǎn**	to go to and fro; round trip

Chinese Characters Writing Practice Pad—**Character #218**

往返船票会便宜很多。

谢谢，两张往返船票。

→ 往返船票会便宜很多。**Wǎngfǎn chuánpiào huì piányi hěn duō.** A round-trip ferry ticket is much cheaper.

→ 谢谢，两张往返船票。**Xièxie, liǎng zhāng wǎngfǎn chuánpiào.** Thank you, two round-trip tickets.

姓

xìng　　surname; family name

女 / 8 strokes

Jaime TAILOR

*His **family name** is Tailor.*

姓名	**xìngmíng**	full name
贵姓	**guìxìng**	What is your surname? (formal)
老百姓	**lǎobǎixìng**	common people
姓氏	**xìngshì**	family name

Chinese Characters Writing Practice Pad—**Character #219**

请问，您贵姓？

免贵姓王。

→ 请问，您贵姓？ **Qǐngwèn, nín guìxìng?**
Excuse me, what is your surname?

→ 免贵姓王。 **Miǎn guì xìng Wáng.** My surname is Wang.

⟍	亅	门	问	问	问	问	问
问							

问 問
Traditional

wèn to ask

门 / 6 strokes

*The lost tourists **asked** for directions.*

问路　　　**wènlù**　　　to ask for directions
提问　　　**tíwèn**　　　to question, to quiz
问候　　　**wènhòu**　　　to greet, to send one's regards to
学问　　　**xuéwèn**　　　learning, knowledge

Chinese Characters Writing Practice Pad—**Character #220**

请代我问候她。

好的。

→ 请代我问候她。 **Qǐng dài wǒ wènhòu tā.**
Please send her my regards.

→ 好的。 **Hǎo de.** Ok.

| ⸜ | ⸜⸜ | ⸜⸜⸜ | 沪 | 沪 | 泮 | 洸 | 洗 |

| 洗 | 洗 | 洗 | 洗 |

洗

xǐ   to wash, to bathe

氵 / 9 strokes

*Dirt got into my eye, and I **washed** it off with water.*

洗澡	**xǐzǎo**	to bathe, to take a shower
洗脸	**xǐliǎn**	to wash the face
干洗	**gānxǐ**	to dry clean; dry cleaning
洗衣机	**xǐyījī**	washing machine

Chinese Characters Writing Practice Pad—**Character #221**

你要快一点洗澡。

再给我一分钟。

→ 你要快一点洗澡。 **Nǐ yào kuài yìdiǎn xǐzǎo.**
 You'd better shower quickly.

→ 再给我一分钟。 **Zài gěi wǒ yì fēnzhōng.**
 Just give me another minute.

| 丿 | 冂 | 月 | 月 | 目 | 目ˊ | 目ˋ | 目ˊ |

| 眼 | 眼 | 眼 | 眼 | 眼 | 眼 | | |

眼

yǎn eye, small hole

目 / 11 strokes

*The house owner peeped through a **small hole** to see who was outside.*

眼睛	**yǎnjīng**	eye
眼镜	**yǎnjìng**	spectacles, glasses
眼泪	**yǎnlèi**	tears
眼光	**yǎnguāng**	eyesight, insight, judgment

Chinese Characters Writing Practice Pad—**Character #222**

你 戴 这 副 眼 镜 很 帅。

女 朋 友 送 的 生 日 礼 物。

→ 你戴这副眼镜很帅。 **Nǐ dài zhè fù yǎnjìng hěn shuài.**
You look great in these glasses.

→ 女朋友送的生日礼物。 **Nǚ péngyou sòng de shēngrì lǐwù.**
It is a birthday gift from my girlfriend.

| 以 | 以 | 以 | 以 | 以 | 以 | 以 | |

以

yǐ

人 / 4 strokes

to use; by means of, according to, in order to

*We **use** a can opener on the tin.*

可以	**kěyǐ**	can, may; possible
因为… 所以…	**yīnwèi...** **suǒyǐ...**	because...therefore...
以为	**yǐwéi**	to suppose; to assume
以便	**yǐbiàn**	so that, so as to

Chinese Characters Writing Practice Pad—**Character #223**

我	以	为	你	不	来	了	。		
这	么	重	要	的	会	议	，	一	定
要	来	。							

→ 我以为你不来了。 **Wǒ yǐwéi nǐ bù lái le.**
I think you will not come.

→ 这么重要的会议，一定要来。 **Zhème zhòngyào de huìyì yídìng yào lái.** Such an important meeting, I must come.

| ↓ | 冂 | 冃 | 因 | 因 | 因 | 因 | 因 |

因

yīn   because of; cause

口 / 6 strokes

Because of the spread
of mosquitoes, there is
an outbreak of diseases.

因此	**yīncǐ**	thus, consequently
原因	**yuányīn**	cause, reason
因而	**yīn'ér**	therefore, as a result
因素	**yīnsù**	element, factor

Chinese Characters Writing Practice Pad—**Character #224**

他 不 来 有 很 多 原 因 。

这 次 可 能 病 了 。

→ 他不来有很多原因。 **Tā bù lái yǒu hěn duō yuányīn.**
He was absent for many reasons.

→ 这次可能病了。 **Zhè cì kěnéng bìng le.**
Maybe he is sick this time.

| 一 | 十 | 十 | 古 | 南 | 自 | 直 | 真 |

| 真 | 真 | 真 | 真 | 真 | | | |

真

zhēn   really, truly, indeed

八 / 10 strokes

*The occurrence of a supermoon is **indeed** an unusual event.*

传真	**chuánzhēn**	to fax; fax
真正	**zhēnzhèng**	genuine, real
天真	**tiānzhēn**	naive, innocent
真实	**zhēnshí**	true, real

Chinese Characters Writing Practice Pad—**Character #225**

这	是	一	个	真	实	的	故	事	。
哇	！	太	感	人	了	。			

→ 这是一个真实的故事。 **Zhè shì yí gè zhēnshí de gùshi.**
This is a true story.

→ 哇！太感人了。 **Wa! Tài gǎnrén le.** Wow, so touching.

ノ	㇗	乍	矢	矢	知	知	知
知	知	知					

知

zhī

矢 / 8 strokes

to know,
to be aware

*Everyone is **to be aware** of traffic when crossing.*

知道	**zhīdào**	to know, to become aware of
通知	**tōngzhī**	to notify, to inform
谁知道	**shuízhīdào**	God knows…, Who would have thought…
知己	**zhījǐ**	bosom friend, confidant

Chinese Characters Writing Practice Pad—**Character #226**

他 是 我 的 知 己。

真 难 得。

→ 他是我的知己。 **Tā shì wǒ de zhījǐ.** He is my bosom friend.
→ 真难得。 **Zhēn nándé.** It's not easy to find one.

纸

纸
Traditional

zhǐ paper

纟 / 7 strokes

*She uses a beautiful **paper** to make cranes.*

剪纸	**jiǎnzhǐ**	to cut paper; papercutting
纸巾	**zhǐjīn**	paper towel, napkin
纸条	**zhǐtiáo**	note, slip of paper
白纸	**báizhǐ**	white paper

可	以	留	张	纸	条	给	他	吗	？
当	然	，		给	你	纸	。		

→ 可以留张纸条给他吗？ **Kěyǐ liú zhāng zhǐtiáo gěi tā ma?**
Can I leave him a note?

→ 当然，给你纸。 **Dāngrán, gěi nǐ zhǐ.**
Of course, here is paper.

W	冂	冃	日	旦	昌	昌	骨
骨	昮	最	最	最	最	最	

最

zuì　　most, the most

日 / 12 strokes

*This bag is considered to be one of **the most** expensive bags.*

最后	**zuìhòu**	last, final; finally
最近	**zuìjìn**	recent; recently
最好	**zuìhǎo**	best; you'd better
最初	**zuìchū**	first, primary, initial

Chinese Characters Writing Practice Pad—**Character #228**

你	最	好	六	月	来	,	五	月	太
冷	。								
六	月	就	可	以	见	面	了	。	

→ 你最好六月来, 五月太冷。 **Nǐ zuìhǎo Liùyuè lái, Wǔyuè tài lěng.** You'd better come in June. It is too cold in May.

→ 六月就可以见面了。 **Liùyuè jiù kěyǐ jiànmiàn le.** Ok, we'll meet in June.

乡	纟	纟	纠	绍	绍	绍
绍	绍	绍				

绍

绍
Traditional

shào
纟 / 8 strokes

to continue,
to carry on, to join

He continues his run in the rain.

介绍　　　**jièshào**　　　to introduce

绍兴酒　　**shàoxīngjiǔ**　wine produced in Shaoxing,
　　　　　　　　　　　　　Zhejiang Province

婚姻介　　**hūnyīn**　　marriage agency
绍所　　　**jièshàosuǒ**

自我介绍　**zìwǒ jièshào**　self-introduction

Chinese Characters Writing Practice Pad—**Character #229**

请 自 我 介 绍 一 下。

我 叫 陈 伟。

→ 请自我介绍一下。 **Qǐng zìwǒ jièshào yíxià.**
Please introduce yourself.

→ 我叫陈伟。 **Wǒ jiào Chén Wěi.** I am Chen Wei.

〈	〈	女	女′	女″	始	始	始
始	始	始					

始

shǐ to begin; then

女 / 8 strokes

*The day **begins** bright and early.*

开始	**kāishǐ**	to start; beginning
始终	**shǐzhōng**	from beginning to end
原始	**yuánshǐ**	original, firsthand
初始	**chūshǐ**	initial

Chinese Characters Writing Practice Pad—**Character #230**

音	乐	剧	就	要	开	始	了	。	
打	出	租	车	去	吧	。			

→ 音乐剧就要开始了。 **Yīnyuè jù jiù yào kāishǐ le.**
The musical is starting soon.

→ 打出租车去吧。 **Dǎ chūzūchē qù ba.** Let's take a taxi.

ヽ	亅	门	冂	间	间	间	间
间	间						

间

間
Traditional

jiān

门 / 7 strokes

between, among;
room

Among the flowers the rose is my favorite.

空间	**kōngjiān**	empty space, room
洗手间	**xǐshǒujiān**	toilet, bathroom
卫生间	**wèishēngjiān**	bathroom
期间	**qījiān**	period of time
中间	**zhōngjiān**	middle

Chinese Characters Writing Practice Pad—**Character #231**

我	想	租	一	套	公	寓	。		
只	有	一	个	洗	手	间	，	行	吗
？									

→ 我想租一套公寓。 **Wǒ xiǎng zū yí tào gōngyù.**
I'd like to rent an apartment.

→ 只有一个洗手间，行吗？ **Zhǐyǒu yí gè xǐshǒujiān, xíng ma?** There is only one bathroom, ok?

| 纟 | 纟 | 纟 | 纠 | 纠 | 纶 | 纶 | 给 |
| 给 | 给 | 给 | 给 | | | | |

给　給
Traditional

1. **gěi**　to, for; to give
2. **jǐ**　to supply, to provide

纟 / 9 strokes

"Please help me **give** this pen to your sister."

送给　**sòng gěi**　to send, to give as a present
给钱　**gěiqián**　to give money
供给　**gōngjǐ**　to furnish, to provide
给予　**jǐyǔ**　to accord, to supply

送给她什么礼物好呢？

她说她想要一盏台灯。

→ 送给她什么礼物好呢？ **Sòng gěi tā shénme lǐwù hǎo ne?**
What present should we give her?

→ 她说她想要一盏台灯。 **Tā shuō tā xiǎng yào yì zhǎn táidēng.** She said she would like a desk lamp.

⺀	⺌	丷	芏	艿	首	首	首
首	首	道	道	道	道	道	

道

dào   road, path; principle

辶 / 12 strokes

*The **road** to our school
is long and winding.*

街道	**jiēdào**	street
道歉	**dàoqiàn**	to apologize
味道	**wèidào**	flavor, taste
道理	**dàolǐ**	reason, argument, principle

Chinese Characters Writing Practice Pad—**Character #233**

您 开 出 租 车 很 久 了 吧 ?

是 ， 我 认 识 每 条 街 道 。

→ 您开出租车很久了吧？ **Nín kāi chūzūchē hěn jiǔ le ba?**
Have you been driving a taxi for a long time?

→ 是，我认识每条街道。 **Shì, wǒ rènshi měi tiáo jiē dào.**
Yes, I know every street.

一	工	工	至	至	至	到	到
到	到	到					

到

dào

刂 / 8 strokes

to (a place), until (a time), up to; to go, to arrive

*The train will **arrive** at 10:00.*

迟到	**chídào**	to arrive late
遇到	**yùdào**	to encounter, to meet
到处	**dàochù**	everywhere
感到	**gǎndào**	to feel, to sense

Chinese Characters Writing Practice Pad—**Character #234**

你	为	什	么	这	么	高	兴	？	
我	遇	到	了	老	朋	友	。		

→ 你为什么这么高兴？ **Nǐ wèishénme zhème gāoxìng?**
Why are you so happy?

→ 我遇到了老朋友。 **Wǒ yùdào le lǎo péngyou.**
I met an old friend.

| 一 | 卄 | 吉 | 吉 | 吉 | 责 | 寿 | 卖 |
| 卖 | 卖 | 卖 | | | | | |

卖　　賣
Traditional

mài　to sell

十 / 8 strokes

*Many websites **sell** things online.*

卖票	**màipiào**	to sell tickets
卖家	**màijiā**	seller
专卖	**zhuānmài**	monopoly, exclusive right to trade
出卖	**chūmài**	to offer for sale, to sell, to betray

Chinese Characters Writing Practice Pad—**Character #235**

在专卖店买的吗？

不是，网上买的。

→ 在专卖店买的吗？ **Zài zhuānmàidiàn mǎi de ma?**
  Did you buy it at the specialty store?

→ 不是，网上买的。 **Búshì, wǎngshàng mǎi de.**
  No, I bought it online.

| 丶 | 八 | 宀 | 灾 | 灾 | 空 | 空 | 穿 |

| 穿 | 穿 | 穿 | 穿 | | | | |

穿

chuān

穴 / 9 strokes

to wear, to put on,
to pass through

*The hiking path **passes**
through waterfalls in
the forest.*

穿衣服	**chuān yīfu**	to put on clothes
穿鞋	**chuānxié**	to put on shoes
看穿	**kànchuān**	see through (a person, scheme, trick etc.)
穿过	**chuānguò**	to pass through

Chinese Characters Writing Practice Pad—**Character #236**

汽车正穿过隧道。

隧道很长。

→ 汽车正穿过隧道。 **Qìchē zhèng chuānguò suìdào.** The bus is passing through a tunnel.

→ 隧道很长。 **Suìdào hěn cháng.** The tunnel is very long.

| 丿 | 𠂉 | 钅 | 钅 | 钅 | 钅 | 钅 | 钅 |
| 错 | 错 | 错 | 错 | 错 | 错 | 错 | 错 |

错

错
Traditional

There is a **mistake**
in the spelling.

cuò   mistake; wrong, bad

钅 / 13 strokes

不错	**búcuò**	not bad, correct
错误	**cuòwù**	mistake; wrong
错字	**cuòzì**	incorrect character
错过	**cuòguò**	to miss (a schedule, an appointment etc.)

Chinese Characters Writing Practice Pad—**Character #237**

这	篇	文	章	有	很	多	错	误	。
好	的	，		我	去	修	改	。	

→ 这篇文章有很多错误。 **Zhè piān wénzhāng yǒu hěn duō cuòwù.** There are a lot of mistakes in this article.

→ 好的，我去修改。 **Hǎo de, wǒ qù xiūgǎi.**
Ok, I will revise it.

| 一 | 丁 | 不 | 不 | 不 | 还 | 还 | 还 |
| 还 | 还 | | | | | | |

还　還
Traditional

1. **hái**　still, yet, also
2. **huán**　to return

辶 / 7 strokes

The bikes **are returned** to the company after the time is up.

还有	**háiyǒu**	furthermore, in addition
还没	**háiméi**	not yet
还书	**huánshū**	to return books
讨价还价	**tǎojià-huánjià**	to bargain, to haggle over prices

便	宜	一	点	儿	吧	？			
不	要	讨	价	还	价	了	。		

→ 便宜一点儿吧? **Piányi yìdiǎnr ba?**
Can you make it cheaper?

→ 不要讨价还价了。 **Búyào tǎojiàhuánjià le.** No bargaining.

一	一	一	西	西	西	�	票
票	票	票	票	票	票		

票

piào　　ticket, ballot

示 / 11 strokes

*What time is this **ticket** for?*

电影票　　**diànyǐng piào**　　cinema ticket
支票　　　**zhīpiào**　　　　bank check
邮票　　　**yóupiào**　　　　postage stamp
股票　　　**gǔpiào**　　　　 shares (of a company)

Chinese Characters Writing Practice Pad—**Character #239**

请	问	怎	么	付	款	？			
你	可	以	交	一	张	支	票	。	

→ 请问怎么付款？ **Qǐngwèn zěnme fùkuǎn?** How can I pay?

→ 你可以交一张支票。 **Nǐ kěyǐ jiāo yì zhāng zhīpiào.**
You can pay by check.

| 丿 | 心 | 忄 | 忄⁻ | 忄⁼ | 忄 | 情 | 情 |

| 情 | 情 | 情 | 情 | 情 | 情 |

情

qíng

忄 / 11 strokes

feeling, sentiment, emotion

After being saved from the flood, this person was full of emotion.

心情   **xīnqíng**   mood, frame of mind

爱情   **àiqíng**   romance, love

感情   **gǎnqíng**   emotion, sentiment, affection

情人节   **Qíngrén jié**   Valentine's Day

Chinese Characters Writing Practice Pad—**Character #240**

你	为	什	么	心	情	这	么	好	？
不	告	诉	你	，		是	秘	密	。

→ 你为什么心情这么好？ **Nǐ wèishénme xīnqíng zhème hǎo?** Why are you in such a good mood?

→ 不告诉你，是秘密。 **Bú gàosu nǐ, shì mìmì.** I'm not telling you, it's a secret.

｀	｀	亠	亠	亠	产	产	旁
旁	旁	旁	旁	旁			

旁

páng

方 / 10 strokes

beside; one side, side

*On **one side** of the table is a standing lamp.*

旁边	**pángbiān**	side; beside
旁人	**pángrén**	other people
路旁	**lùpáng**	roadside
旁听	**pángtīng**	to sit-in (a class, trail)

Chinese Characters Writing Practice Pad—**Character #241**

路	旁	有	个	卖	羊	肉	串	的	。
我	们	去	尝	尝	。				

→ 路旁有个卖羊肉串的。 **Lùpáng yǒu gè mài yángròuchuàn de.** There's a lamb kebab stall on the roadside.

→ 我们去尝尝。 **Wǒmen qù chángchang.** Let's go try it.

| 一 | 艹 | 艹 | 艻 | 药 | 药 | 药 | 药 |
| 药 | 药 | 药 | 药 | | | | |

药

藥
Traditional

yào　　medicine, drug

艹 / 9 strokes

Medicine can be in tablet form and in liquids.

中药	**Zhōngyào**	Chinese medicine
西药	**Xīyào**	western medicine
药店	**yàodiàn**	pharmacy, chemist
药片	**yàopiàn**	pill or tablet (medicine)

Chinese Characters Writing Practice Pad—**Character #242**

请	问	，		附	近	有	药	店	吗	？
药	店	就	在	超	市	对	面	。		

→ 请问，附近有药店吗？ **Qǐngwèn, fùjìn yǒu yàodiàn ma?**
Excuse me, is there a pharmacy nearby?

→ 药店就在超市对面。 **Yàodiàn jiù zài chāoshì duìmiàn.**
The pharmacy is just opposite the supermarket.

㇀	乆	女	奶	奶	奶	奶	奶

奶

nǎi   milk

女 / 5 strokes

*Chocolate **milk** is yummy!*

牛奶	**niúnǎi**	milk
奶奶	**nǎinai**	grandma
奶酪	**nǎilào**	cheese
酸奶	**suānnǎi**	yogurt

Chinese Characters Writing Practice Pad—**Character #243**

我	买	了	一	些	奶	酪	。		
噢	，	味	道	很	特	别	。		

→ 我买了一些奶酪。 **Wǒ mǎi le yìxiē nǎilào.**
I bought some cheese.

→ 噢，味道很特别。 **Ō, wèidao hěn tèbié.**
Well, the taste is very special.

| 丿 | 冂 | 冊 | 冊 | 罒 | 甲 | �!黑 | 黒 |

| 黒 | 黑 | 黑 | 黑 | 黑 | 黑 | 黑 | |

黑

hēi   black, dark, evil

黑 / 12 strokes

*Some children are
afraid of the **dark**.*

黑板	**hēibǎn**	blackboard
黑眼睛	**hēiyǎnjīng**	black eyes
黑夜	**hēiyè**	dark night
乌黑	**wūhēi**	pitch-black, dark

Chinese Characters Writing Practice Pad—**Character #244**

黑	板	上	写	着	"	禁	止	吸	烟
"	。								
对	不	起	，	没	注	意	。		

→ 黑板上写着 "禁止吸烟"。 **Hēibǎn shàng xiě zhe "jìnzhǐ xīyān".** "No Smoking" on the black board.

→ 对不起，没注意。 **Duìbuqǐ, méi zhùyì.**
Sorry, I didn't notice it.

件

jiàn piece (measure word),
亻 / 6 strokes a document

*This quilt is made
of different **pieces**
of cloth.*

条件	**tiáojiàn**	conditions, circumstances, terms
软件	**ruǎnjiàn**	software
信件	**xìnjiàn**	letter
附件	**fùjiàn**	attachment (to email, SMS)

Chinese Characters Writing Practice Pad—**Character #245**

你	写	的	文	章	呢	？			
在	电	邮	的	附	件	里	了	。	

→ 你写的文章呢？ **Nǐ xiě de wénzhāng ne?**
Where is your article?

→ 在电邮的附件里了。 **Zài diànyóu de fùjiàn lǐ le.**
In the attachment of the email.

丿　匚　乍　牙　乐　乐　乐　乐

乐　樂
Traditional

1. **lè**　happy, cheerful; joy
2. **yuè**　music

丿 / 5 strokes

*Music brings **joy** and cheer to the listeners.*

音乐	**yīnyuè**	music
音乐会	**yīnyuèhuì**	concert
乐队	**yuèduì**	band, pop group
俱乐部	**jùlèbù**	club
快乐	**kuàilè**	happy, merry

Chinese Characters Writing Practice Pad—**Character #246**

| 他 | 有 | 一 | 个 | 乐 | 队 | 。 | | | |

| | | | | | | | | | |

| | | | | | | | | | |

| | | | | | | | | | |

| 我 | 去 | 看 | 他 | 们 | 的 | 演 | 唱 | 会 | 。 |

| | | | | | | | | | |

| | | | | | | | | | |

| | | | | | | | | | |

→ 他有一个乐队。 **Tā yǒu yí gè yuèduì.** He has a band.

→ 我去看他们的演唱会。 **Wǒ qù kàn tāmen de yǎnchànghuì.** I am going to their concert.

门

门
門
Traditional

mén　gate, door

门 / 3 strokes

*They have a strong **gate** at the front of their house.*

门口	**ménkǒu**	doorway, gate, exit
出门	**chūmén**	to go out, to leave home, to go on a journey
专门	**zhuānmén**	specialty
门诊	**ménzhěn**	outpatient service

这	个	超	市	专	门	卖	水	果	。
水	果	超	市	很	受	欢	迎		。

→ 这个超市专门卖水果。 **Zhège chāoshì zhuānmén mài shuǐguǒ.** This supermarket sells only fruit.

→ 水果超市很受欢迎。 **Shuǐguǒ chāoshì hěn shòu huānyíng.** The fruit supermarkets are very popular now.

| ﹀ | ﹁ | 亠 | 亠 | 立 | 立 | 音 | 音 |
| 音 | 音 | 意 | 意 | 意 | 意 | 意 | 意 |

意

yì

心 / 13 strokes

idea, meaning, thought

*What is the **meaning** of this sign?*

满意　**mǎnyì**　satisfied, satisfactory
愿意　**yuànyì**　willing
注意　**zhùyì**　to take note of, to pay attention to
生意　**shēngyì**　business

Chinese Characters Writing Practice Pad—**Character #248**

愿	意	和	我	去	看	京	剧	吗	？
非	常	愿	意	。					

→ 愿意和我去看京剧吗？ **Yuànyì hé wǒ qù kàn jīngjù ma?**
Are you willing to watch Beijing Opera with me?

→ 非常愿意。 **Fēicháng yuànyì.** Yes, most certainly.

氵	氵	氵	氵	沪	沪	泳	泳
泳	泳	泳					

泳

yǒng   swimming; to swim

氵 / 8 strokes

*They love **swimming** in the sea.*

游泳	**yóuyǒng**	swimming; to swim
泳衣	**yǒngyī**	swimsuit
泳镜	**yǒngjìng**	swimming goggles
泳池	**yǒngchí**	swimming pool
蝶泳	**diéyǒng**	butterfly stroke

Chinese Characters Writing Practice Pad—**Character #249**

我	的	泳	镜	丢	了	。			
是	不	是	忘	在	泳	池	了	？	

→ 我的泳镜丢了。 **Wǒ de yǒngjìng diū le.** I lost my goggles.

→ 是不是忘在泳池了？ **Shìbúshì wàng zài yǒngchí le?**
  Did you leave it in the pool?

| 𠃌 | 𫝀 | 饣 | 饦 | 馆 | 馆 | 馆 | 馆 |
| 馆 | 馆 | 馆 | 馆 | 馆 | 馆 | | |

馆

館
Traditional

guǎn　building, shop

饣 / 11 strokes

*This **building** is the National Library.*

宾馆	**bīnguǎn**	guesthouse, lodge
大使馆	**dàshǐguǎn**	embassy
博物馆	**bówùguǎn**	museum
科学馆	**kēxuéguǎn**	science museum

Chinese Characters Writing Practice Pad—**Character #250**

你 住 哪 个 宾 馆 ?

我 住 青 年 旅 社 。

→ 你住哪个宾馆? **Nǐ zhù nǎge bīnguǎn?**
Which guesthouse you staying at?

→ 我住青年旅社。 **Wǒ zhù qīngnian lǚshè.**
I am staying in a youth hostel.

| 一 | 丁 | 下 | 下 | 正 | 正 | 正 | 正 |

正

zhèng

止 / 5 strokes

straight, upright, proper, main

*This old lady sits **upright** in her chair.*

正常	**zhèngcháng**	regular, normal
正好	**zhènghǎo**	just (in time), just right
正确	**zhèngquè**	correct, proper
正式	**zhèngshì**	formal, official

Chinese Characters Writing Practice Pad—**Character #251**

喂	，	我	正	好	要	去	找	你	。
有	什	么	事	吗	？				

→ 喂，我正好要去找你。 **Wèi, wǒ zhènghǎo yào qù zhǎo nǐ.**
Hey, I'm just going to look for you.

→ 有什么事吗？ **Yǒu shénme shì ma?** What about?

行

1. **xíng** to go, to walk
2. **háng** row, profession

彳 / 6 strokes

行李箱	**xíngli xiāng**	suitcase
银行	**yínháng**	bank
自行车	**zìxíngchē**	bicycle
一行	**yì háng**	one row
流行	**liúxíng**	popular, in vogue
旅行	**lǚxíng**	to travel; journey

Ms Ashley is a teacher by profession.

Chinese Characters Writing Practice Pad—**Character #252**

你	的	行	李	箱	怎	么	那	么	重
？									
旅	行	时	买	的	纪	念	品	。	

→ 你的行李箱怎么那么重？ **Nǐ de xíngli xiāng zěnme nàme zhòng?** Why is your suitcase so heavy?

→ 旅行时买的纪念品。 **Lǚxíng shí mǎi de jìniànpǐn.** I bought a lot of souvenirs when traveling.

丿	冂	月	目	且	助	助	助
助	助						

助

zhù   to help, to assist

力 / 7 strokes

*This walker **helps** the old man keep his balance.*

辅助	**fǔzhù**	to assist, to aid
助手	**zhùshǒu**	assistant, helper
助理	**zhùlǐ**	assistant
自助	**zìzhù**	self-service, self-served

我	想	和	您	谈	一	下	计	划	。
请	和	我	的	助	理	预	约	时	间
。									

→ 我想和您谈一下计划。 **Wǒ xiǎng hé nín tán yíxià jìhuà.**
I would like to talk with you about the plan.

→ 请和我的助理预约时间。 **Qǐng hé wǒ de zhùlǐ yùyuē shíjiān.** Please make an appointment with my assistant.

一	二	云	云	运	运	运	运
运	运						

运　運
Traditional

yùn
辶 / 7 strokes

to move, to transport, to use

*The ambulance **transports** the sick person to hospital quickly.*

命运	**mìngyùn**	fate, destiny
幸运	**xìngyùn**	lucky; luck
运气	**yùnqi**	luck (good or bad)
运用	**yùnyòng**	to use, to put to use

能	找	到	光	盘	就	好	了	！	
我	们	碰	碰	运	气	吧	。		

→ 能找到光盘就好了！ **Néng zhǎodào guāngpán jiù hǎo le.**
It would be good if we could find the CD.

→ 我们碰碰运气吧。 **Wǒmen pèngpeng yùnqi ba.**
Let's try our luck.

⌄	⊓	口	⼫	乃	员	员	员
员	员						

员

員
Traditional

yuán
口 / 7 strokes

person, employee,
member

*He is an **employee**
of this hotel.*

服务员　　**fúwùyuán**　　　waiter, waitress

售货员　　**shòuhuòyuán**　salesperson

演员　　　**yǎnyuán**　　　　actor or actress,
　　　　　　　　　　　　　　　　performer

员工　　　**yuángōng**　　　　staff, employee

Chinese Characters Writing Practice Pad—**Character #255**

现在售货员越来越少。

快递员就越来越多。

→ 现在售货员越来越少。 **Xiànzài shòuhuòyuán yuèláiyuè shǎo.** Now the number of salespeople is declining.

→ 快递员就越来越多。 **Kuàidìyuán jiù yuèláiyuè duō.** The number of couriers is growing.

一 丁 丆 石 石 石 石 石

石

shí rock, stone

石 / 5 strokes

*The big **rock** prevents
entry into the cave.*

石头	**shítou**	stone
钻石	**zuànshí**	diamond
石榴	**shíliu**	pomegranate
化石	**huàshí**	fossil
石油	**shíyóu**	oil, petroleum

Chinese Characters Writing Practice Pad—**Character #256**

化	石	是	怎	样	形	成	的	？	
我	也	不	太	清	楚	。			

→ 化石是怎样形成的？ **Huàshí shì zěnyàng xíngchéng de?**
How are fossils formed?

→ 我也不太清楚。 **Wǒ yě bú tài qīngchu.**
I am not too sure.

| ㄱ | ㄱ | 已 | 已 | 已 | 已 | |

已

yǐ　　already; to stop

己 / 3 strokes

*It is **already** 9 P.M.
but no one is home
to eat dinner.*

已经	**yǐjīng**	already
早已	**zǎoyǐ**	long ago
不得已	**bùdéyǐ**	to act against one's will, to have no alternative
而已	**éryǐ**	that's all

Chinese Characters Writing Practice Pad—**Character #257**

年	轻	人	喜	欢	上	网	购	物	。
是	，		不	得	已	才	去	商	店
									。

→ 年轻人喜欢上网购物。 **Niánqīngrén xǐhuan shàngwǎng gòuwù.** Young people love online shopping.

→ 是，不得已才去商店。 **Shì, bùdéyǐ cái qù shāngdiàn.** Yes, they only go to the stores when they have no choice.

| 丨 | 口 | 吕 | 咼 | 吊 | 疋 | 足 | 趴 |

| 趴 | 路 | 路 | 路 | 路 | 路 | 路 | 路 |

路

lù　　road

足 / 13 strokes

*We travel on country **roads** using this type of transportation.*

马路	**mǎlù**	street, road
公路	**gōnglù**	highway, road
路口	**lùkǒu**	crossing, intersection
路线	**lùxiàn**	itinerary, route

Chinese Characters Writing Practice Pad—**Character #258**

我	要	去	美	国	自	驾	游	。	
自	己	设	计	路	线	吗	？		

→ 我要去美国自驾游。 **Wǒ yào qù Měiguó zìjiàyóu.**
  I am doing a self-drive tour in the United States.

→ 自己设计路线吗？ **Zìjǐ shèjì lùxiàn ma?**
  Do you design your own itinerary?

丿	亻	仁	什	休	休	休	休
休							

休

xiū

亻 / 6 strokes

to rest, to stop doing something for a period of time

*She took a **rest** after reading too much.*

休息	**xiūxi**	rest; to rest
退休	**tuìxiū**	to retire; retirement
休闲	**xiūxián**	leisure, relaxation
休假	**xiūjià**	to be on leave; vacation

Chinese Characters Writing Practice Pad—**Character #259**

大城市生活的压力大。

我希望有休闲时间。

→ 大城市生活的压力大。 **Dà chéngshì shēnghuó de yālì dà.**
There is more pressure living in big cities.

→ 我希望有休闲时间。 **Wǒ xīwàng yǒu xiūxián shíjiān.**
I wish I could have leisure time.

| 丶 | 亠 | 立 | 立 | 立 | 立 | 亲 | 亲 |
| 亲 | 亲 | 新 | 新 | 新 | 新 | 新 | 新 |

新

xīn　　new; newly

斤 / 13 strokes

*After the dental visit, her teeth look **new**.*

新闻	**xīnwén**	news
新鲜	**xīnxiān**	fresh (experience, food etc.); freshness
重新	**chóngxīn**	again, afresh
创新	**chuàngxīn**	to innovate

Chinese Characters Writing Practice Pad—**Character #260**

我	把	书	重	新	读	了	一	遍	。
有	的	书	不	能	只	读	一	遍	。

→ 我把书重新读了一遍。 **Wǒ bǎ shū chóngxīn dú le yí biàn.**
I read the book again.

→ 有的书不能只读一遍。 **Yǒu de shū bù néng zhǐ dú yí biàn.**
For some books, you can't just read them once.

| 𠂉 | 𠂉 | 𠂉 | 𠂉 | 𠂉 | 𠂉 | 𠂉 | 竺 |
| 笋 | 笑 | 笑 | 笑 | 笑 | | | |

笑

xiào　　to laugh, to smile

⺮ / 10 strokes

*This nurse **smiles** when she talks.*

微笑	**wēixiào**	smile
大笑	**dàxiào**	to laugh heartily
笑脸	**xiàoliǎn**	smiling face
嘲笑	**cháoxiào**	to laugh at, to ridicule

Chinese Characters Writing Practice Pad—**Character #261**

他	说	话	总	是	带	着	微	笑	。
他	很	友	善	。					

→ 他说话总是带着微笑。 **Tā shuōhuà zǒngshì dài zhe wēixiào.** He always smiles while he speaks.

→ 他很友善。 **Tā hěn yǒushàn.** He is friendly.

丶 丿 为 为 为 为 为

为　為
Traditional

1. **wéi**　to act as
2. **wèi**　because of, for, to

丶 / 4 strokes

Because it is dark,
she has the light on.

为了	wèile	in order to, for the purpose of, so as to
以为	yǐwéi	to suppose, to assume
成为	chéngwéi	to become
作为	zuòwéi	to regard as; achievement

Chinese Characters Writing Practice Pad—**Character #262**

我	以	为	你	会	打	车	来	。	
上	下	班	的	时	候	骑	车	快	。

→ 我以为你会打车来。 **Wǒ yǐwéi nǐ huì dǎchē lái.**
 I thought you would be taking a taxi.

→ 上下班的时候骑车快。 **Shàngxiàbān de shíhou qí chē kuài.**
 During the rush hours, cycling can be much faster.

一	二	干	王	王`	玕	玗	玩
玩	玩	玩					

玩

wán to play, to have fun

王 / 8 strokes

The children have fun playing together.

开玩笑	**kāiwánxiào**	to make fun of, to crack a joke
玩具	**wánjù**	plaything, toy
玩弄	**wánnòng**	to play with, to toy with
好玩儿	**hǎowánr**	amusing, fun, interesting

Chinese Characters Writing Practice Pad—**Character #263**

不	要	给	孩	子	太	多	玩	具	。
我	完	全	同	意	你	的	想	法	。

→ 不要给孩子太多玩具。 **Búyào gěi háizi tài duō wánjù.**
Don't give children too many toys.

→ 我完全同意你的想法。 **Wǒ wánquán tóngyì nǐ de xiǎngfǎ.**
I totally agree with you.

丿	夕	夕	外	外	外	外	外

外

wài

夕 / 5 strokes

outside; in addition; foreign, external

In addition to a passport, you may need a visa too.

另外	**lìngwài**	another; in addition, besides
外婆	**wàipó**	mother's mother, maternal grandma
此外	**cǐwài**	besides, in addition
外交	**wàijiāo**	diplomacy; diplomatic
意外	**yìwài**	accident; unexpected

Chinese Characters Writing Practice Pad—**Character #264**

校	长	送	给	我	一	张	照	片	！
你	一	定	很	意	外	吧	？		

→ 校长送给我一张照片！ **Xiàozhǎng sòng gěi wǒ yì zhāng zhàopiàn.** The principal gave me a photograph!

→ 你一定很意外吧？ **Nǐ yídìng hěn yìwài ba?** Weren't you surprised?

跳

tiào　　to jump, to hop

足 / 13 strokes

To get to the opposite side, you need to jump over this drain.

跳舞	**tiàowǔ**	to dance
跳远	**tiàoyuǎn**	long jump
跳高	**tiàogāo**	high jump
心跳	**xīntiào**	heartbeat

Chinese Characters Writing Practice Pad—**Character #265**

一演讲我就心跳加快。

放松才能讲好。

→ 一演讲我就心跳加快。 **Yí yǎnjiǎng wǒ jiù xīntiào jiākuài.**
My heartbeat increases whenever I make a speech.

→ 放松才能讲好。 **Fàngsōng cái néng jiǎng hǎo.**
Relax and you will be fine.

⺌	日	日	日	旦	昂	昆	是
是	是	是	题	题	题	题	题

題

题

Traditional

tí

页 / 15 strokes

topic, matter for discussion, exam question

*I could not answer one of the **exam questions** today.*

问题	**wèntí**	question, problem
题目	**tímù**	subject, title, topic
难题	**nántí**	difficult problem
主题	**zhǔtí**	theme, subject
标题	**biāotí**	title, heading, headline

Chinese Characters Writing Practice Pad—**Character #266**

文	章	的	标	题	很	吸	引	人	。
确	实	很	好	。					

→ 文章的标题很吸引人。 **Wénzhāng de biāotí hěn xīyǐn rén.**
The topic of the article is very attractive.

→ 确实很好。 **Quèshí hěn hǎo.** Really good.

㇂	厂	斤	斤	斤	所	所	所
所	所	所					

所

suǒ

斤 / 8 strokes

actually; place, that which

*That **place** gives me the creeps.*

所以	**suǒyǐ**	therefore, as a result
厕所	**cèsuǒ**	toilet, lavatory
场所	**chǎngsuǒ**	location, place
派出所	**pàichūsuǒ**	local police station

Chinese Characters Writing Practice Pad—**Character #267**

怎	么	这	么	早	来	上	班	？	
搭	顺	风	车	，		所	以	早	了	。

→ 怎么这么早来上班？ **Zěnme zhème zǎo lái shàngbān?**
How come you are at work so early?

→ 搭顺风车，所以早了。 **Dā shùnfēngchē, suǒyǐ zǎo le.**
I got a lift so I came early.

`	``	``	``	关	关	关	送
送	送	送	送				

送

sòng

辶 / 9 strokes

to deliver, to carry, to give

*A bouquet of lovely roses **was delivered** to me on Valentine's Day.*

送人	**sòngrén**	to see someone off
送礼	**sònglǐ**	to give a present
寄送	**jì sòng**	to send, to transmit
赠送	**zèngsòng**	to present as a gift

Chinese Characters Writing Practice Pad—**Character #268**

明	天	我	们	到	机	场	送	你	。
我	会	哭	的	。					

→ 明天我们到机场送你。 **Míngtiān wǒmen dào jīchǎng sòng nǐ.** Tomorrow we will see you off at the airport.

→ 我会哭的。 **Wǒ huì kū de.** I'll cry.

手

手

shǒu   hand, (formal) to hold

手 / 4 strokes

*The worker accidentally hurt his **hand**, and it is now in bandages.*

左手	**zuǒshǒu**	left hand, left-hand side
手机	**shǒujī**	cell phone
分手	**fēnshǒu**	to part company, to split up, to break up
手套	**shǒutào**	glove, mitten

Chinese Characters Writing Practice Pad—**Character #269**

女朋友和他分手了。

难怪他那么伤心。

→ 女朋友和他分手了。 **Nǚ péngyou hé tā fēnshǒu le.**
His girlfriend broke up with him.

→ 难怪他那么伤心。 **Nánguài tā nàme shāngxīn.**
No wonder he is so sad.

試
Traditional

试

shì   to test, to try

讠 / 8 strokes

*He **tries** the car before he buys it.*

试题	**shìtí**	exam question, test topic
试卷	**shìjuàn**	examination paper, test paper
尝试	**chángshì**	to try; attempt
面试	**miànshì**	to interview; interview

| 我 | 要 | 去 | 参 | 加 | 一 | 个 | 面 | 试 | 。 |
| 你 | 准 | 备 | 好 | 了 | 吗 | ？ | | | |

→ 我要去参加一个面试。**Wǒ yào qù cānjiā yí gè miànshì.**
I am going to attend an interview.

→ 你准备好了吗？**Nǐ zhǔnbèi hǎo le ma?**
Are you prepared?

身

shēn body, oneself

身 / 7 strokes

*His **body** is frail, so he needs a walker.*

身体	**shēntǐ**	the body
健身	**jiànshēn**	to exercise, to keep fit
身边	**shēnbiān**	at one's side, on hand
身份	**shēnfèn**	identity, status, capacity

Chinese Characters Writing Practice Pad—**Character #271**

朋	友	一	直	陪	在	我	身	边	。
你	很	幸	运	。					

→ 朋友一直陪在我身边。 **Péngyou yìzhí péi zài wǒ shēnbiān.**
My friend was with me all the time.

→ 你很幸运。 **Nǐ hěn xìngyùn.** You are very lucky.

一	一	一	写	写	写	写	事
事	事	事					

事

shì   matter, thing, item

亅/ 8 strokes

*"I have an **item** to declare," said the traveler.*

事情	**shìqing**	affair, matter, thing
故事	**gùshi**	narrative, story, tale
从事	**cóngshì**	to go for, to engage in
军事	**jūnshì**	military affairs

Chinese Characters Writing Practice Pad—**Character #272**

我	老	师	特	别	会	讲	故	事	。
我	也	选	她	的	课	。			

→ 我老师特别会讲故事。 **Wǒ lǎoshī tèbié huì jiǎng gùshi.**
My teacher is very good at storytelling.

→ 我也选她的课。 **Wǒ yě xuǎn tā de kè.**
I will choose her class as well.

𠃍	夕	刍	刍	刍	色	色	色
色							

色

sè   color

⺈ / 6 strokes

*Use the **color** pencils to make your drawing beautiful.*

红色	**hóngsè**	red
绿色	**lǜsè**	green
颜色	**yánsè**	color
景色	**jǐngsè**	scenery, scene, landscape
色彩	**sècǎi**	tint, coloring, coloration

Chinese Characters Writing Practice Pad—**Character #273**

我家乡的景色很迷人。

我今年就去看看。

→ 我家乡的景色很迷人。 **Wǒ jiāxiāng de jǐngsè hěn mírén.**
The landscape of my hometown is very charming.
→ 我今年就去看看。 **Wǒ jīnnián jiù qù kànkan.**
I will visit your hometown this year.

让　让　让　让　让　让　让

让

讓
Traditional

ràng　　to yield, to permit,
讠 / 5 strokes　　to let sb do sth

*The parent **permits** his
son to take up fencing*

让路　**rànglù**　　　to make way
让开　**ràngkāi**　　　to get out of the way, to step aside
让步　**ràngbù**　　　to concede; concession
转让　**zhuǎnràng**　　to transfer; transfer

Chinese Characters Writing Practice Pad—**Character #274**

爷	爷	一	点	儿	也	不	让	步	。
让	我	去	和	他	谈	谈	。		

→ 爷爷一点儿也不让步。 **Yéye yìdiǎnr yě bú ràngbù.**
Grandpa is not giving in at all.

→ 让我去和他谈谈。 **Ràng wǒ qù hé tā tántan.**
Let me talk to him.

千

qiān thousand

十 / 3 strokes

```
  999
+   1
1,000
```

*Add 1 to 999, and
you have a **thousand**.*

千年	**qiānnián**	millennium
千万	**qiānwàn**	ten million, countless; one must by all means
秋千	**qiūqiān**	swing, seesaw
千方百计	**qiānfāng bǎijì**	by all means, by every possible way

Chinese Characters Writing Practice Pad—**Character #275**

她	千	方	百	计	地	想	离	开	。
为	什	么	？						

→ 她千方百计地想离开。 **Tā qiānfāng-bǎijì de xiǎng líkāi.**
She was trying to get out of here by all means.

→ 为什么？ **Wèishénme?** Why?

猫　貓
Traditional

māo　cat

犭 / 11 strokes

熊猫	**xióngmāo**	panda
猫眼	**māoyǎn**	peephole
猫头鹰	**māotóuyīng**	owl
猫步	**māobù**	catwalk

Many people like to have
a Lucky **Cat** at home.

Chinese Characters Writing Practice Pad—**Character #276**

不要随便开门。

好，我先从猫眼看看。

→ 不要随便开门。 **Búyào suíbiàn kāi mén.**
Don't just open the door.

→ 好，我先从猫眼看看。 **Hǎo, wǒ xiān cóng māoyǎn kànkan.**
Alright, I will check from the peephole first.

`	亠	亠	亠	亠	亠	亠	京
京	虻	就	就	就	就	就	

就

jiù

九 / 12 strokes

at once,
right away

*The boy obeyed **at once** when
he saw that his mom was angry.*

成就	**chéngjiù**	accomplishment, success, achievement
将就	**jiāngjiu**	to accept (a bit reluctantly), to put up with
就是	**jiùshì**	precisely, exactly
就业	**jiùyè**	to get a job, to start a career

Chinese Characters Writing Practice Pad—**Character #277**

没 有 热 水 怎 么 洗 澡 呀 ？

就 一 晚 ， 将 就 一 下 吧 ！

→ 没有热水怎么洗澡呀？ **Méiyǒu rèshuǐ zěnme xǐzǎo ya?**
How can I take a shower without hot water?

→ 就一晚，将就一下吧！ **Jiù yì wǎn, jiāngjiu yí xià ba!**
For one night, just put up with it.

| ⺜ | ⺧ | ⺍ | 牛 | 生 | 告 | 告 | 告 |

| 告 | 告 | | | | | | |

告

gào
口 / 7 strokes

to say, to tell,
to announce

*The latest news **was
announced** just a
few minutes ago.*

转告	**zhuǎngào**	to pass on, to communicate
广告	**guǎnggào**	to advertise; advertisement
告别	**gàobié**	to leave, to bid farewell to
报告	**bàogào**	to inform; report

Chinese Characters Writing Practice Pad—**Character #278**

他	就	要	小	学	毕	业	了	。	
要	和	好	朋	友	告	别	了	。	

→ 他就要小学毕业了。 **Tā jiùyào xiǎoxué bìyè le.**
He will graduate from primary school.

→ 要和好朋友告别了。 **Yào hé hǎo péngyou gàobié le.**
He will say goodbye to his good friends.

| ✐ | 丿 | 斤 | 斤 | 斤 | 辶斤 | 近 | 近 |
| 近 | 近 | | | | | | |

近

jìn

辶 / 7 strokes

near, close to, approximately

*The church is **close to** the post office.*

附近	**fùjìn**	(in the) vicinity, nearby
近来	**jìnlái**	recently, lately
近期	**jìnqī**	near (in time), in the near future, very soon, recent
接近	**jiējìn**	to approach, to get close to

你 近 来 好 像 瘦 了 很 多 。

我 每 天 运 动 一 小 时 。

→ 你近来好像瘦了很多。 **Nǐ jìnlái hǎoxiàng shòu le hěn duō.**
You seem to have lost a lot of weight recently.

→ 我每天运动一小时。 **Wǒ měitiān yùndòng yì xiǎoshí.**
Yes, I do exercise for an hour every day.

但

丿 丨 仃 但 但 但 但 但

但 但

但

dàn but

亻 / 7 strokes

*There is a lot of food **but** I don't like any of them.*

虽然… **sūirán…dànshì…** although…(but)…
但是…

不但… **búdàn…érqiě …** not only…but also…
而且…

Chinese Characters Writing Practice Pad—**Character #280**

它	不	但	好	看	而	且	便	宜	。
是	的	。							

→ 它不但好看而且便宜。 **Tā búdàn hǎokàn érqiě piányi.**
It is not only pretty but also cheap.

→ 是的。 **Shì de.** Yes.